GLIMPSES OF
THE HARVARD PAST

Glimpses of the Harvard Past

BERNARD BAILYN

DONALD FLEMING

OSCAR HANDLIN

STEPHAN THERNSTROM

HARVARD UNIVERSITY PRESS

Cambridge, Massachusetts, and London, England 1986

Library of Congress Cataloging in Publication Data
Main entry under title:

Glimpses of the Harvard past.

   1. Harvard University—History—Addresses, essays,
lectures. 2. Universities and colleges—Massachusetts—
Cambridge—History—Addresses, essays, lectures.
I. Bailyn, Bernard.
LD2151.G56 1986   378.744'4   85-14131
ISBN 0-674-35443-5 (alk. paper)

Preface

Midway into its fourth century, Harvard University pauses to mark the way it has come in the past, as well as to peer toward the road ahead of it. This little volume aims to contribute to a sharper perspective of the retrospective view, in the hope of thereby clarifying the possibilities for the future.

The essays here assembled are far from constituting a history of the University. The felt, but as yet unfilled, need for such an account induced the Charles Warren Center for Studies in American History, in the academic year 1970–71, to offer a cooperative, non-credit voluntary course on Harvard's history. Senior members of the Department of History then delivered the lectures, each addressing topics within his own field of interest. The participants did not aim at comprehensive coverage, nor did they adopt a uniform approach. They hoped only to provide sample glimpses of a past still significant in the twentieth century, for while much changed in the life of the institution, some elements endured. These lectures proved successful enough to justify repetition in subsequent years. Expanded and revised, they form the substance of this book.

The full history remains to be written, to complete Samuel Eliot Morison's magisterial volumes on the seventeenth century. Rich materials for subsequent years remain untapped; and they bear upon every aspect of the economic, social, intellectual, and religious history of the United States. Some day they will attract a pen worthy of the subject. In the interim, these glimpses of the Harvard past may arouse the curiosity of readers and stimulate thought about why the University came to be what it is in the 1980s.

Oscar Handlin

Contents

Illustrations

GLIMPSES OF
THE HARVARD PAST

BERNARD BAILYN

Foundations

Harvard's development over 350 years has been enormously rich and complex—full of interest for social and intellectual history, for the history of scholarship, science, pedagogy, and politics. And full of questions—questions, for example, concerning the social history of the student body—its recruitment, social characteristics, and subsequent careers—and questions concerning the faculty. We know something, statistically, about the social sources and destinies of the graduates over the first century of the College's existence, but little of the later generations. And we know something too of the careers of the faculty, especially of the great figures of the nineteenth century: Peirce, Royce, and Santayana; Agassiz, Gray, and Wyman; Child and Kittredge; Wendell and the two Nortons; Taussig, Gay, and Adams. But others too once strode the Yard like giants, and we know very little about them. Among the historians: Torrey, Gurney, Emerton, and Gross were men of achievement, forgotten now, whose creative efforts helped shape the evolution of historical studies everywhere. And there were once-famous figures who contributed nothing to scholarship or science but who dominated the lives of innumerable cohorts of students. Silas Marcus McVane, for example: his mind, a colleague was obliged to report in an official history, was "slow working," and he was "one of the dullest lecturers that ever addressed a class. His dismal monotonous delivery, broken by periods of prayer-like silence with closed eyes, took all the life out of his students." His one "flash of genius" was to devise a system of scheduling examination groups; for which signal achievement, it was believed (nothing else suggested itself), he was honored in 1887 by elevation to the McLean chair of Ancient and Modern History, which he occupied, to the misery of undergraduates, for no less than twenty-four years.

Among the professorial ministers, there were men of genius—or if not of genius then of steady and notable achievement—or if not of notable achievement, then of sustained productivity—or at the very least of moral probity; they were all, minimally, exemplars of Christian virtues. Except, apparently, the Rev. Samuel Locke (class of 1755), President of the University 1770–1773, whose term of office came to an abrupt end when a maid in Wadsworth House (then the president's residence) was discovered to be in a delicate condition.

Of the presidents, the major figures are well known: Dunster, Chauncy, Leverett, Holyoke, Kirkland, Quincy, Eliot, and their distinguished twentieth-century successors. But we know little of other less luminous presidents: dutiful, hard-working men like James Walker (1853–1860). A forceful preacher whose meaty sermons were spiced with prophetic aphorisms, Walker was crippled with arthritis, but continued the ancient presidential practice of patrolling the Yard at night with a lantern to be sure all the students were safely confined. And though deaf and, in S. E. Morison's words, "totally devoid of aesthetic sense," he presided over the introduction of music into the curriculum.

Harvard's benefactors are no less interesting a group, and their contributions made all else possible. William Stoughton, class of 1650, was the first person to donate a building to an American college. His Stoughton "College," built in 1699, stood, until it was torn down in 1781, between Massachusetts and Harvard Halls, forming Harvard's first quadrangle. Stoughton, who had trained for the ministry but drifted into politics, was lieutenant governor of Massachusetts and also a judge—in fact one of the three judges who sentenced twenty people to death for witchcraft in 1692, and the only one who never repented of the deed. In his superbly stark portrait, which

Five presidents, 1861 (left to right: Josiah Quincy, 1829–1845; Edward Everett, 1846–1849; Jared Sparks, 1849–1853; James Walker, 1853–1860; Cornelius Felton, 1860–1862).

James Russell Lowell [right] and Sir Leslie Stephen at Elmwood, 1885.

shows his building in the background, this implacable Puritan hanging judge appears as rigid and formally posed as a pharaoh, his long, pale, somewhat pained face resolute, full of grim determination and righteousness. It is perhaps appropriate that this arresting portrait, a monitory tale in itself, now hangs over the main entrance of the graceful Georgian meeting room in University Hall where the Faculty of Arts and Sciences conducts its deliberations.

The buildings themselves are data for a remarkable story that has at last been told: a story almost as long as Harvard's entire history. It stretches from the first Harvard Hall (1638–1677) and the Indian "College," an Elizabethan building erected in 1655 on the site of the present Matthews Hall and demolished in 1698, to the early provincial Georgian of Massachusetts Hall (1720) and the gem-like Holden Chapel (1744), to Bulfinch's neoclassical University Hall (1815) to Richardson's romanesque Sever Hall (1880) and to the Le Corbusier, Yamasaki, and Stirling buildings of our own time. Apthorp House and Elmwood, the two wooden domestic buildings of the 1760s taken over by Harvard, still gleam in the sun as they did two hundred years ago. But they have witnessed strange scenes. Apthorp House, now the residence of the master of Adams House, was denounced by the local Cantabrigians as a "bishop's palace" and almost stormed when it was built for the rich Anglican preacher East Apthorp. Later it served as a genteel jail for General Burgoyne and his fellow officers captured in the battle of Saratoga. As for Elmwood, its builder and first owner, the loyalist merchant Thomas Oliver, ended up in 1774 cowering with his family behind the mansion's front door to escape the fury of a mob determined to force his resignation from the royal council. Two generations later James Russell Lowell, who was born in the house and lived there most of his life, entertained his friend Leslie Stephen there. Neither ever forgot the enjoyment they found in each other's company at Elmwood. In Lowell's study, Noel Annan has written,

> the two men would sit, attired in velvet jackets and puffing at
> pipes, hour after hour, submerged in an intimate silence to be
> broken by a comment on some point which would lead to a
> barrowload of volumes, scored with pencil marks, being scat-
> tered over the floor in search of a reference . . . [Lowell] was the
> kind of scholar Stephen could admire, tossing hay in the

3

meadow by morning, knowing every bird and flower by name, revelling in Yankee speech and drinking whiskey-toddy by night. Grunts of pleasure greeted Lowell's jocular verse and erudite puns, and when the visit ended they parted with a long, strong handshake at the corner of the road under the lamp which both men looked back to with emotion till the end of their days. (*Leslie Stephen*, 1984, p. 55)

Later still Professor Arthur Kingsley Porter, who bought Elmwood in 1925, worked on his innovative books and lectures on the history of art and architecture in the same study that Lowell and Stephen had used. Restored with great care to its ideal appearance in the 1770s, Elmwood, now the official residence of the University's President, remains a masterpiece of unostentatious provincial elegance, and while it is no longer surrounded by the ninety acres that once were part of the estate, its broad lawn still conveys something of the spaciousness of the original setting.

The students, the faculty, the benefactors, the buildings—all are part of the history of North America's oldest non-governmental institution, but only part. Harvard's financial history, the course of its involvement with the local community, its contributions to scholarship, science, letters, and the public welfare—all of this too forms part of the story. The question is what to select from this plethora, and where to begin.

Let us start at the beginning and concentrate on formative developments.

Why was Harvard founded, and with what expectations? What do we know of its foundations and of the shaping effect of these foundations on the University's growth and character? What permanent disposition and style were generated in the founding years, built into the institution's structure at the start?

These are simple questions, but they have proved to be hotly debated issues in the University's history, and the terms of the controversy, the answers that have been given, have been persistently misconceived.

The debate over the character of Harvard's founding, its essential character, purpose, and style, began within seventy years of the founding. Cotton Mather (class of 1678), that remorseless busybody, that long-winded guardian of Puritan virtues, smarting from the insult of his father's being dropped from the presidency in 1701, served up the first historical interpretation of the College's founding. Fearful of the liberalizing influence of the likes of John Leverett, a lawyer, he insisted that Harvard had been founded as "a College of Divines" and had become a "Happy *Seminary*," a seedbed of ministers and Godly magistrates, in the direct line of succession from the schools of the prophets. In its pristine years, under President Charles Chauncy (1654–1672)—whom the Mathers, admiringly if somewhat hysterically, called "Charlemagne" and (after Theodore of Beza) the "gymnasiarch"—the College had been full of the Sons of the Prophets. There was no telling what betrayal would result if heedless latitudinarians like Leverett had their way. Harvard, in the heart of what Cotton Mather called, in Hebrew, the *"Kirjath-Sepher"* (the City of Books [Josh. 15:15]—that is, Cambridge, Massachusetts) might just as well be handed over to the Bishop of London.

A century later the same controversy erupted in a new form. Orthodox Congregationalists insisted that Harvard had been founded as "a theological institution" devoted to perpetuating the Puritans' distinctive form of Protestant Christianity. Liberal Unitarians, who controlled the College after 1805, thought differently, and leapt upon evidence such as Harvard's absolute refusal, from the start, to impose exclusionary oaths on its members, to prove the College's broadly liberal origins.

A century later still a similar dispute took sharper, more learned, better documented form. A new "liberal" view emerged as part of the reassessment of Puritanism carried out by a triumvirate of Harvard historians: Kenneth Murdock, Perry Miller, and above all Samuel Eliot Morison, whose four-volume *Tercentennial History of Harvard College and University* is a masterpiece of institutional history. Morison was never in doubt about the reason for Harvard's founding. It was to provide a broad liberal education for young gentlemen and scholars, a proposition Morison could easily document by uncovering seventeenth-century Harvard's close connections with the broad world of humane letters. Of course, Morison wrote, Harvard was a religious college too, but "emphatically not a 'divinity school' or a seminary for the propagation of puritan theology—although the

Mathers would have made her just that . . . Harvard was founded, and in the seventeenth century supported, as a college of English university standards for the liberal education of the young men of New England, under strict religious discipline." And he quoted President Urian Oakes's characterization of his third graduating class, that of 1677, as *"liberi liberaliter educati"* (gentlemen educated like gentlemen), a phrase repeated by Perry Miller in dedicating to Morison his anthology of Puritan writings (1938).

Morison's *Tercentennial History* was magnificently authoritative. But doubt was not stilled and the ancient views were far from obliterated. Within three years of the publication of the Tercentennial volumes, the learned journal *Church History* carried an article by a leading scholar entitled "The Morison Myth of the Founding of Harvard." In it Morison's belief that Harvard was created "to provide for the broad *liberal* education of young gentlemen and scholars" was denounced as a dangerous myth that "threatens to do irreparable damage to the historical reconstruction of the period" as Morison's "faulty conclusions" wind their insidious way into the "textbooks and . . . classrooms of the nation." Morison suffered, the writer said, from a double affliction. He was a Harvard professor, which was bad enough, since it predisposed him to find a replica of the modern university in the early college; but in addition he had little sympathy with the Puritans' concept of religion. In its origins Harvard College, the writer concluded, "was little more than a theological seminary, thrust into existence by a desire for trained ministerial leadership in a society wherein the clergy held a position of paramount importance in matters civil as well as spiritual."

The doubts that Harvard's original purpose had been the advancement of general secular learning and the liberal training of gentlemen went even deeper than that. From within the *"Kirjath-Sepher"* itself—indeed from a study in Widener Library, and from the pen of no less an authority than the incumbent of Harvard's oldest endowed chair, the Hollis Professorship of Divinity (1721)—came the most contrary commentary of all. In a formidable paper, "Translatio Studii: The Puritans' Conception of Their First University in New England, 1636," Professor George Williams returned to the thought of the Mathers and reconstructed a cosmic, divinely heroic, account of Harvard's origins as seen by those second- and third-generation

Puritans for whom the College's founding was a near-contemporary event. Far from being created to educate young gentlemen liberally, Harvard, to theologians like the Mathers, Professor Williams pointed out, had originally been conceived of as a major step in the world-historical, immemorial *translatio studii*. It had been a beachhead on this pagan continent, launched by a task force of Christian militia charged with the divine obligation of forwarding the providential transfer of God's learning from land to land and people to people. The New England Puritans, Professor Williams wrote, "had participated epochally in the transfer of learning to the New World," and Harvard, the "corporate heir of all the ages in the communication of *Veritas*," had been their vehicle.

The idea of Puritan Harvard as a happy seminary,

> through whose precincts flowed the rivers of Eden before the fall, irrigated now by the streams of divine grace through Christ the Second Adam, or alternatively as a school of the prophets, in continuous succession with the great schools of Christendom from old English Cambridge and medieval Paris . . . back to Athens, back further to the imagined schools of the prophets to Paradise before Adam's fall, cannot be overemphasized if we wish to understand the power and purposefulness which the great idea of the providential *translatio studii*, the transfer of learning in orderly succession from Paradise to the new seminary in the wilderness of the New World, gave to the builders of the first center of learning in New England.

And Professor Williams went on to discuss in detail the Mathers' conception of Harvard's professors as prophets and of its students as "militia Christi on the frontier of faith and reason." To be sure, he admitted, "most of this university lore is now muted in the archives of Harvard and of the many colleges founded by various Protestant denominations in imitation of the first English-Speaking American University." But "the Puritan adaptation of the medieval *translatio studii* in terms of the disciplined seminary of the wilderness has been a powerful if largely hidden impetus in the rise of American higher education."

So the controversy over Harvard's origins has proceeded, focussed on the question of religion. But the differences on this issue can be easily reconciled. Harvard at its founding and through the colonial years was not a modern liberal arts college or university writ small; but neither was it a divinity school devoted to producing preachers of a certain persuasion. The percentage of preachers among the seventeenth-century alumni—about 50 percent—correctly represents the original balance of interests. Harvard was founded as an institution from which the leadership of church, state, and trade was expected to emerge, and that leadership, like the community as a whole, was expected to remain deeply and correctly Christian. There was no choice between secular learning and religious learning. The curriculum was indeed secular in many aspects, as Morison said, but the overall orientation was religious. "Youth at the college," John Eliot wrote, "are brought up for the holy service of the Lord either in magistracy or ministry especially." Secular learning was well nourished at Harvard College in the early years, but it was dedicated to Christian goals as defined by the Puritans—that is, free of the corruptions of prelacy, empty ritual, and human vanity that, they believed, had so bedeviled the English universities.

And indeed in this connection one can see Harvard as the essence of the central theme of the whole Puritan exodus of the early seventeenth century—the idea of the saving remnant. With corruption believed to be settling everywhere in England, and especially in those seedbeds of the future, the universities, hope could survive only if a stalwart band withdrew into the wilderness and there set up an institution that would perpetuate the Truth. Protestant circles throughout Europe understood that, like the Massachusetts settlement itself, the College was to be a spearhead of an innovating movement at the heart of great affairs in England and the Netherlands. It made sense in 1641 for the New Englanders to invite the Moravian reformer Comenius to become Master of Harvard. But by then the English Civil War had disrupted the old regime in England and energies there could focus on reform of the ancient universities. In that process, and through the rest of the seventeenth century, New England in general and Harvard in particular became a provincial backwater; by Cotton Mather's time the city on the hill had become parochial and provincial. This context renders the struggle between the Mathers and the liberals led by John Leverett more understandable. Both sides sought the same goal, to bring Harvard back into the mainstream of the greater, outer world. But the Mathers saw that world in terms of the heroic Puritan past and Leverett saw it in the liberalizing culture then developing in Britain and western Europe.

This is the substance of the classic controversy over the religious element in the founding of Harvard. "Veritas," used first in 1643 but adopted as the standard Harvard motto only in the mid-nineteenth century, was God's truth. It was not considered different in spirit from the two seventeenth-century mottos: *In Christi gloriam* (on the seal of the 1650 charter) and *Christo et ecclesiae* (in the draft charter of 1692). Secular knowledge was valued, and assumed to be necessary for men of all modes of life. But in the end it was an intensely religious, ascetic Puritan culture that created this institution and that carried it through precarious years into the stability of the eighteenth century.

All of this is historically important, but not particularly mysterious, and it does not explain the College's permanent characteristics, its persistent character, structure, and style. These subtler and enduring elements in the story of Harvard's origins emerge from the observation of anomalies: that is, of gaps, peculiarities, and inconsistencies which do not explain themselves. To see such anomalies one must start with a picture of what a predictable straight-line development would have been for an informed person at the time. What would Harvard have been like if all the normal expectations of 1636 had been fulfilled? The answer is, a replica of a seventeenth-century English college, particularly Emmanuel College of Cambridge University, founded by Puritans as an improvement over its parent institution, Christ's College, which they believed had been corrupted. This expectation was no vague thing. There were at least 130 Oxford and Cambridge alumni among the settlers by 1646—one to every 30 or 35 families. Of the 43 men in the General Court of 1636 who founded Harvard, fifteen were either themselves graduates of English universities or sons or brothers of graduates.

For them a college was a residential unit of students and masters who lived on the income of endowments (usually land rents) created at first by an original benefactor, a man like Sir Walter Mildmay, who endowed Emmanuel College (1584), which sent over 35 alumni to Massachusetts. These "hard money" endowments were owned and the institution ruled by the master and fellows, who formed a Corporation—a self-governing property-owning institution; but they were also the teachers. These property-owning teachers together with a specified number of students formed the College, which was legally and functionally different from the University. The University, which was also chartered, had two special characteristics. First, it had other and "higher" faculties than the "philosophical" faculty, that is, the Faculty of Arts and Sciences. The colleges taught only up through the first two degrees and in arts and sciences; the universities had separate faculties in medicine and law. And the university had degree-granting powers together with an appropriate examination system. The university and not the colleges awarded degrees, from the B.A. to the doctorate. So even Trinity College Dublin, which has been called the last of the medieval universities and the first of the colonial, was chartered by Queen Elizabeth in 1592 as an isolated college, but it was expected to become, in the words of its charter, a *"mater universitatis"*—the core unit of an eventual University of Dublin.

The founders of Harvard were educational conservatives. They were not attempting to create new forms of education. Yet in fact they did. And the pattern they extemporized proved to be permanent, and a model for American institutions of higher education.

The major, structural innovations fall into two main groups, both of which emerged amid great terminological confusion.

For over a century there was no certainty in the popular name or the characterization of the institution created in 1636. The charter of 1650, under which Harvard is still governed, refers to "Harvard College," but the people who knew the place did not call it that. Sometimes they called it the College in Cambridge, sometimes the University (though Harvard acquired medical instruction only in the 1780s and a law school only in 1815). Sometimes it was called Cambridge University or even Cambridge College. The temporary charter of 1692 called it a "Colledge or Academy." To make things even more confused, individual buildings, later called Halls, were then called "colleges." So, "Harvard College" could mean either the institution as a whole or a particular building in the institution. The edifice donated in 1699 by Judge Stoughton was never called anything but Stoughton "College"; the Indian dormitory of 1655 too was called a "College."

*William Stoughton, with Stoughton Hall
in the background, 1700.*

Most of these confusions in terminology arose from the peculiar urgencies of the founding. The founders wanted to create a *college*; that is, a residential and instructional unit of masters and students. But they needed the degree-granting powers of a university, that is, a recognized guild of masters and students. The Massachusetts General Court created a collegiate corporation in the charter of 1650, though by what authority is not clear, but it did not confer degree-granting powers or even vaguely refer to the College as a *"mater universitatis."* The powers of a university were simply assumed, in 1642, when the first bachelors' degrees were conferred. The short-lived second charter of 1692 recognized the problem by empowering the Corporation "to grant and admit to Academical Degrees, as in the Universities in England." And to demonstrate the College's university status President Increase Mather, who had written the charter, had the Corporation immediately confer a doctorate—on himself, for his many books and "because he had rendered himself for his Learning and Merits, the object of highest commendation, not only among the American, but among the European Churches." Though the charter of 1692 was disallowed by the Privy Council, the degree-granting powers it conferred and that the College had assumed in 1642 survived without challenge. By the early eighteenth century Harvard's bachelor degrees were recognized by Oxford, and the issue was beyond contention. But in the founding period it was difficult to know what to call Harvard: a college, yes; but a university, somewhat mysteriously, also.

And the "Harvard" element was an artifact. John Harvard was not a founder as Mildmay or John Balliol had been. There was no individual founder, though the Puritans eagerly sought for one. The founder of the institution was the Massachusetts legislature, which in 1636 granted £400 to construct a college building. Subsequently, John Harvard left his library and half his estate to what the legislators had created. No English college had been created by a legislature, and none was sustained by the community as Harvard was. The College was largely supported in the seventeenth century by the income from the Charlestown ferry and by a tax levied by the General Court to pay the salary of the president. And in fact Harvard, like all Massachusetts institutions of higher education, was supported by the state well into the nineteenth century. For "public" and "private" were not distinctive terms then. Harvard College, though an independent corporation, was originally created as a public institution, and was governed as such for almost two hundred years.

This background was of great and permanent importance in shaping the modern institution. For it meant, first, that Harvard's central core, from the beginning, was a single undergraduate college of liberal arts and sciences; the other faculties, the graduate schools, have been additions to this collegiate foundation. As a result, the Faculty of Arts and Sciences has been, and remains, the central element in the University, despite the University's present size and complexity and despite the importance of the professional faculties. It is distinct, in this, from many other modern universities—from Johns Hopkins, for example, which began as a graduate school and later acquired a college, or from Columbia, which added a separate faculty when it created a graduate school of arts and sciences. And second, since the University's undergraduate students form a single collegiate unit, instruction to all has been, and is, handled by a single body of teachers and is equally available to all. This has remained so as the College has grown to the size of the entire multi-collegiate universities of Cambridge and Oxford.

The House system did not alter this basic fact. The Houses were created as residential conveniences with only informal educational functions; they were never intended to be units of formal instruction that differed in the character of their staffs, in their interests, in their educational capacities, and in their wealth. It was the Faculty, through its academic departments, and not the Houses, that alone had—and has—the capacity to set and maintain instructional standards and to train students properly in the various disciplines. The Houses' functions are to encourage and develop education informally, as part of daily living; to provide personal guidance, proper accommodations, and studying facilities; to enhance the non-academic aspect of students' lives; and to help unify and sophisticate the disparate groups that enter the College. Hence the founding of Churchill College in Cambridge University after World War II was entirely different from the founding of Mather House, at approximately the same time. It was consistent with the structure of Cambridge University that Churchill should have its own staff of instructors and its own endowment, that it should admit people to the University, and that it should have its own instructional program with its own emphasis, in science. Harvard is still, in curricular terms, a single college, which admits undergraduate students into a single instructional system. For over three centuries the College—though it has academically incorporated a once loosely associated women's annex, though it has grown to equal the size of the ancient English universities, and though it has spawned thirteen residential sub-units—has remained a *single* and *unified* educational entity, which still constitutes the heart of the greater University.

The terminological confusion of the seventeenth and eighteenth centuries was thus created by the problem of establishing a viable English college in this peculiar setting, a problem that resulted ultimately in a distinctive form of university college.

But that was not the most profound change that took place. A second and more complex development transformed both the governance of the College and its relation to the outside world—at no one's desire and only after bitter fights that threatened to destroy the institution.

At the start no one thought very much about the question of governance. The assumption was that this college would be like other English colleges, namely, a residential teaching institution where the teachers were the governing and property-owning corporation. But there was trouble at the start. Since there were no Fellows in the beginning, control was taken, first, by a temporary committee of the General Court and then, in 1642, by a board of trustees (Overseers) composed of magistrates and of ministers from the surrounding towns. The Overseers, an external board, were to administer the property as an unincorporated public trust, and were responsible to the General Court which had appointed them. But the belief persisted that when the infancy of the institution was over, it would revert to the familiar form of self-government in which the teachers comprised a governing corporation. So the charter of 1650 created a corporation in traditional form as a distinctive governing body, consisting of a president, a treasurer, and five fellows, and it vested the ownership of the property in them. These individuals were, in law, the College; as a corporate body they were to teach, hire employees, and make rules for the institution. But the Overseers remained in the charter; they were expected to supervise the College's finances, to exercise a veto power over actions of the Corporation, to perform an arbitration function within the College, and above all to perpetuate the association of the College and the state. It was expected that their immediate governing powers would be transferred to the traditional corporation when that body was sufficiently mature.

But the simple transfer of governing power from this original external board to the residential teaching faculty did not take place as expected. Nothing that happened, in fact, was simple. The history of the relations between Overseers and Corporation for almost two centuries is a story of Byzantine complexity—full of labyrinthine maneuvers, legal complexities, and bewildering political struggles. A transfer of corporate powers did eventually take place, but only much later, when the Corporation had entirely changed its character.

It seemed from the very start that something was wrong with the resident teachers. They should have been eminent scholars and divines willing to spend their lives as Fellows of the Corporation, as their British counterparts did. And indeed there were such men of intellectual distinction in New England, men well qualified to perform the teaching functions within the College and able too to handle the practical affairs of a property-owning corporation—Thomas Hooker, for example, Samuel Mather, John Cotton, or Roger Williams. The 130 Oxford and Cambridge alumni and the eight graduates of other European universities in New England before 1646 held among them no less than 154 university degrees: 87 B.A.s, 63 M.A.s, 3 B.D.s, and 1 M.D. But in fact the eminent New England scholars did not become Fellows of Harvard College. Instead the teachers in the seventeenth century proved to be young men, in their early twenties, fresh B.A.s waiting the traditional three years for the M.A. degree, most of them unmarried and inexperienced. And their tenures were extremely short. The tutors in the seventeenth century served in the College for an average term of two and one half years before going on to ministerial appointments in the New England towns. Four months after its charter was granted, four of the five Harvard Fellows had left. For at least a full century, the faculty was largely composed of young men who would later be described as teaching fellows, and seldom were more than two such tutors at work in the College at one time. The teaching in the seventeenth century was largely done by the president, with a succession of transient assistants, thirty-seven in all, who were made Fellows of the Corporation during their tenures as teachers. But some of the Corporation Fellows of the period were *former* tutors who had left the College for other work but had retained their Fellowship rights; and there were others on the board who had never been teachers.

This strange, confused, and unexpected development resulted, first, from the financial situation that persisted through most of the colonial period. There was a total lack of substantial endowments. The College lived from hand to mouth, on gifts from the General Court and from individuals. And this meant that the manner of life within the College was hardly appropriate for men of the dignity of English university Fellows. More important in this frontier society, preachers and scholars of true eminence found important public roles open to them, and they resisted devoting themselves to the affairs of the struggling College. Increase Mather put the point precisely when he faced a choice of giving up either the Harvard Presidency or his Boston ministry. "What?" he asked. "Should I leave off preaching to 1500 souls . . . to expound to 40 or 50 children, few of them capable of edification by such exercises?" So throughout the first half century the positions on the Corporation were often unfilled and the transfer of authority from the Board of Overseers to the Corporation was stalled. And then in 1684 everything was thrown into turmoil when the English government annulled the colony's charter and along with it the College's. Harvard's legal existence became a matter of grave doubt as failing efforts were made to obtain a Crown charter or to have the General Court rewrite the charter of 1650 along new lines.

Stability was restored only in 1708, with the appointment of President John Leverett, when the original corporation charter was declared in effect. By then the basic questions were pressing for solution. Should corporate ownership be vested in the youthful, transient hands of the teachers? If the answer were yes, other questions immediately followed. Would the rights of Fellows follow the teachers when they left the College? Would their replacements, by virtue of taking on teaching duties, automatically acquire the powers of corporate Fellows? It seemed reasonable to say no to these questions—to say that the teachers would not be Fellows. For if they were, and soon left, they would be out of touch with the College after their short terms of service, and if there were to be nonresident Fellows, far more dignified, able, and intellectually powerful non-teachers might be appointed than those who had taught briefly at the College.

The confusion grew. Some teachers were appointed with no relationship to the governing boards, and no particular titles were attached to them. They were simply tutors. But some teaching appointments were associated with the Fellowship of the Corporation, and the individuals thus appointed were known as Fellows of the Corporation. Still others were appointed as Fellows, but not Fellows of the Corporation, and hence were called Fellows of the House. The confusion was further compounded by religious and political alignments that fell into place behind those who urged a return to the traditional residential corporation of teachers and those who declared that tradition inapplicable and argued for continuing the governance of an external lay board supervised by Overseers who expressed the public's interest in the institution.

In 1716–17 President Leverett forced the issue into the open. He supported the Corporation in electing to its membership three non-teachers, and then hired two tutors, on three-year teaching contracts, who would have no expectation of becoming members of that board. By then four of the five Fellows were non-residents, and the principle that the teachers should be appointed to the Corporation was being deliberately defied. One of these tutors, Nicholas Sever, took his case to the Overseers, claiming that as a teacher in Harvard College he automatically deserved to become a Fellow of the Corporation. The controversy deepened and spread. The orthodox Congregational group, which controlled a majority in the colony's House of Representatives, saw the relevance of Sever's cause to their interests and backed him. The Governor and Council backed Leverett and the Corporation. Petitions flew left and right, hearings were held—by the Corporation, by the Overseers, by the House, by the Council. A distinction between Fellows and tutors, Sever claimed, was unwarranted, unhistorical, "a thing entirely new under the sun." Clearly, the Corporation replied, the charter had given them, and no one else, the right to manage funds and promulgate laws for the College, leaving the execution of them to the President and tutors. Such powers, of finance and governance, would hardly have been left in the hands of "younger gentlemen of small experience." Everything would be in order, they concluded, if the tutors "would, as become Christians, study to be quiet and do their own business."

When the dust settled and all the arguments were exhausted, the Council's view prevailed. Tutors would *not* automatically become Fellows of the Corporation, though as a political compromise Sever was appointed to that board, along with another tutor and the new Hollis Professor, Edward Wigglesworth. This expedient mixture in the membership of the Corporation persisted for a full generation thereafter, but the distinction in principle between the teachers and the Corporation had been firmly established, and in time the distinction in fact became settled. In 1780 the last tutor left the Corporation, in 1806 the last professor.* The Corporation thereafter consisted predominantly of lawyers, ministers, and businessmen, all quite capable of exercising effectively the legal power they held under the charter; none were resident teachers. By then, the Corporation had edged the Overseers aside and had become the effective owners and directors of the College, leaving the Overseers with supervisory powers similar to those envisioned in 1650 and with the all-important role of associating the College with the legislature of the state, hence of perpetuating its public character.

Thus from the earliest years, Harvard was ultimately governed and its property owned by a board of distinguished non-teachers—at first the Overseers, then the Corporation, but the Corporation only when it had changed its character from a collegiate organization of teachers to a board of external directors: external, that is, to the

---

* In the subsequent 180 years there have been a few exceptions. Joseph Story was not only an Associate Justice of the U.S. Supreme Court during most of his term as Fellow of the Corporation (1825–1845) but Dane Professor of Law as well; James Walker was Alford Professor of Natural Religion, Moral Philosophy, and Civil Polity during most of his years on the Corporation (1834–1853); and Ephraim Gurney was University Professor of History when he served on the Corporation (1884–1886). A century passed before another such concurrent appointment was made. In 1985 Henry Rosovsky, Geyser University Professor and former Dean of the Faculty of Arts and Sciences, was elected to the Board.

fellowship of teachers, the "immediate government," as it was then called, the faculty and administration as it is now known.

This development was not accidental, a mere peculiarity of historical forces present in Puritan New England and of the clash of personalities in the early eighteenth century. Significantly, the same creation of dual boards and the same eventual dominance of external lay control also developed in the second American college, William and Mary, founded in Virginia by the Church of England in 1693. And with the founding of Yale (1701) the ambiguities ceased to exist. Yale made no pretense of imitating an English collegiate institution. It was governed by an external lay board from its inception, and the same has been true of the many hundreds of colleges and universities founded in the United States in the two centuries that followed.

Harvard was the progenitor of this form of governance, for reasons that lay deep in the structure of American life. The pattern of external lay control, ambiguously but definitively set by Harvard, stemmed from the root impulse that accounted for the founding of the institution in the first place. The pattern here was not that of medieval Europe, where masters and students came together to serve their guild needs in scholarship and teaching and then were incorporated for protection from the society around them. In its inception Harvard was an artifact of the community as a whole, and the form of governance that developed allowed the community to retain control of its own creation and not simply to follow the dictates of the scholars and teachers within it.

Harvard, and after it all American colleges and universities, has never been an academic ivory tower—never isolated from the world around it, as English colleges, at least in the eighteenth century, were. Harvard has always been closely related to, and indeed in the legal control of, the outside world, and responsive to it. The ultimate constituency has changed: it is now the vast alumni body tied into American society at large in a thousand ways. At times this external lay control created problems for the immediate government, though never as severe as they might have been. But this close relationship of college and society prevented Harvard from ever becoming the agency of a self-enclosed professoriate. And it guaranteed the vitality of the institution, financially and otherwise, as nothing else could possibly have done.

Hollis Hall, room 5, in 1887.

BERNARD BAILYN

Why Kirkland Failed

This title is deliberately paradoxical. John Thornton Kirkland (A.B. 1789, President 1810–1828), a Unitarian minister, was the most popular, the most beloved president Harvard has ever had. He was a man of extraordinary charm, an easy and witty conversationalist, sensible, humane, tolerant, endlessly cheerful, open to change, devoted to his responsibilities and to the College in all its aspects. A "complete gentleman in his manners," wrote one of his first students, he "aimed to treat the students as gentlemen that, if possible he might make them so." They responded to his treatment of them with devotion, and they never forgot the attractiveness of his personality and the genial atmosphere of Harvard under his leadership. He had no children of his own, and seems to have adopted, emotionally, the entire undergraduate body through the eighteen years of his presidency. Years later worldly men of great accomplishment and sophistication who had passed through the College under his aegis—George Bancroft; the literary critic George Ripley—spoke of him in rhapsodies of praise and admiration. His memory evoked in them the best of their carefree, energetic youth and mingled with their earliest hopes and aspirations.

Yet he was no populist, no panderer to boys' and young men's tastes. He was always dignified, always instructive, always high-minded, though never pedantic or heavily intrusive. His mixture of dignity and geniality, his witty good cheer, and his undefinable charm that relaxed and attracted everyone he met were as effective with adults as with students—and they had wonderful results for the College. A Federalist conservative, he was close to Boston's business community and solicitous of their interests. They responded generously and supportively, even in the final debacle.

No one, until close to the end, could have imagined that his administration would close disastrously, with bitter recrimination; that this charming and popular president would in effect be hounded out of office, insultingly, abusively, by one or more members of the Corporation.

For quite aside from his personal attractiveness, the objective accomplishments of his years as president were extraordinary. With the support of such powerful members of the Corporation as John Lowell, Harrison Gray Otis, Judge Joseph Story, and Chief Justice Theophilus Parsons, and with continuing subsidies from the state of Massachusetts, he expanded the financial base of the College, adding, besides unrestricted funds, fifteen endowed, or partly endowed, chairs. He transformed the appearance of the College, partly by adding new buildings: Holworthy Hall (1812), Divinity Hall (1825), and above all University Hall (1815) (porticoed in its original appearance), which contained four dining rooms (commons) on the ground floor, one for each class, and on the second floor a chapel (the present faculty room), recitation rooms, and offices. No less important, he cleaned up the inner Yard (the present Tercentenary Theater, between Widener Library and Memorial Church), which before his time was a hodgepodge of pig pens, sheep commons, breweries, and scattered privies. In this noisy, smelly dump area, he built a neat row of new privies ("university minor," the students called it) behind a screen of newly planted pine trees, cleaned out the rest of the mess, and planted elms, lawns, and regular paths. The effect of the new buildings, and especially University Hall, which became the spatial focus of the Yard, was to shift the physical orientation of the College. Earlier, it had formed an open quadrangle, formed by Harvard Hall, Stoughton "College," and Massachusetts Hall facing out to the Cambridge Common. By 1815, with the original Stoughton "College" gone and University Hall built deep within the Yard, and with new Stoughton and Holworthy forming the corner of a new quandrangle facing east toward University Hall, the College had turned inward, away from the town and into itself. The shift was completed years later when the Johnson Gate was built, separating the Yard from the town definitively, and when Thayer and Weld Halls were added on either side of University Hall, completing the inner line.

Kirkland's physical reorientation of the College, shifting it inward and opening the way to the construction of a second, interior Yard, was accompanied by a reorientation of another kind. In his time, and at his desire, the recruitment of the student body shifted. The College broadened out from its exclusively New England and northeastern base. More and more students came from other regions of the country—from the Middle States, and especially from the South. Catholics from Maryland appeared, along with young aristocrats from Virginia and South Carolina, and planters' sons from the Gulf states and the Mississippi Delta, all mixing with country boys from New England farm towns and with the sons of upper class Boston and New England wealth generally. At the start of Kirkland's presidency, only 11 percent of the freshmen came from outside New England; a decade later the proportion was 27 percent.

The result was a growing worldliness and social sophistication in the student body, a variety and social complexity matched by a growing intellectual sophistication. The atmosphere of Kirkland's Harvard was relaxed, liberal, free-thinking, intellectually adventurous and stimulating, an environment ideally suited for the development of young men like Ralph Waldo Emerson, Henry Thoreau, Benjamin Peirce, George Bancroft, Oliver Wendell Holmes, Charles Sumner, and Wendell Phillips. This amiable, sophisticated, and stimulating atmosphere was partly the result of Kirkland's personal nurturing of a witty literary ambience. Partly too it was the result of the growing post-graduate element in the University (the Faculty of Medicine dated back to the 1780s, but the Divinity School was created in 1819, and the Law School was founded in 1817, two years after the creation of the Royall Professorship of Law). And to some extent too it was the result of the appearance of a new generation of professorial scholars among the faculty, especially four famous German-trained scholars, encouraged—indeed subsidized and hired—by Kirkland: Edward Everett, Joseph Cogswell, George Bancroft, and George Ticknor.

Harvard under Kirkland was thus extraordinarily successful—expanding financially, physically, socially, and intellectually. And yet Kirkland's administration ended disastrously. In 1827, under severe pressure from the Corporation, Kirkland suffered a stroke; when he recovered, he was forced to resign. As a result, his years as president are difficult to classify.

It is safe to say that there have been three truly great presidents of Harvard before the twentieth century—great in the sense that they personally turned the institution in new and creative directions, strengthened it substantially, and left a permanent and distinctive mark on its development. The first was Henry Dunster (1640–1654), who guaranteed the wilderness college's survival and created its basic institutional shape. The second was John Leverett (1708–1724), who transformed Harvard from an ingrown, provincial, third generation Puritan institution, uncertain in its organization, into a stable college, open to the world, involved in the major currents of eighteenth-century culture, and who broke with the English collegiate tradition that joined governance with teaching. The third was Charles William Eliot (1869–1909), who built around a genteel university college, still close to the eighteenth century, a powerful modern university in which the advancement of science and scholarship would flourish. These creators or innovators, each in his turn, were followed by consolidators, sustainers, and integrators, of exceptionally long tenures in office: Charles Chauncy (1654–1672); Edward Holyoke (1737–1769); and A. Lawrence Lowell (1909–1933). Kirkland's administration was not greatly creative in the sense that Eliot's or Leverett's was, nor simply enlarging and consolidating as Holyoke's and Chauncy's were. Its quality was distinctive, unique—and elusive. It attempted, rather blindly, with no clear plan or design, without even intending to do so, to bridge an outmoded past and an undefined future—and, not surprisingly, in the end it failed. Given this unacknowledged and only vaguely perceived goal, the question is less why Kirkland ultimately failed than why and how he succeeded as well and as long as he did.

He was beset by three systematic disjunctions in the foundations

John Thornton Kirkland, 1770–1840.

A recitation.

An examination.

of Harvard's life, three sets of problems that demanded resolution but that had no obvious or even practical solutions at the time. The first relates to the curriculum, which had successfully resisted change for a century. The twelve terms of scheduled instruction (three each year) consisted of thirty-three subjects taken in prescribed sequence through the four years. They included various stages of study in ancient languages; mathematics through analytic geometry, trigonometry, and differential calculus; history; English grammar; philosophy (logic, moral, and "intellectual"); elementary physics, chemistry, and astronomy; political economy; and Bible study. But these were less subjects to be explored than books to be conquered. "Astronomy" meant nothing more nor less than some study of passages in John Gummere's *An Elementary Treatise on Astronomy* (1822); political economy meant examining selections from J. B. Say's *Catéchisme d'economie politique* (1803; trans. 1821); the philosophy of natural history meant William Smellie's two-volume work of that title (1790, 1799); history meant A. F. Tytler's *Elements of General History, Ancient and Modern* (1801); and geometry meant a special Harvard translation (1819) of A. M. Legendre's *Eléments de géométrie . . .* (1794). Two famous books—William Paley's *View of the Evidences of Christianity* (1794) and Joseph Butler's *Analogy of Religion, Natural and Revealed, to the Constitution and Course of Nature* (1736)—formed senior-year subjects in themselves. And a four-volume textbook, compiled at Harvard from French sources by Professor John Farrar and entitled *The Cambridge Course of Natural Philosophy*, was the set text in two courses in the sophomore year (analytic geometry and topography), three in the junior year (calculus, mechanics, and electricity and magnetism), and one in the senior year (optics).

It is true that a few substitutes were allowed at the beginning of the junior year (math or a language, ancient or modern, could be substituted for Hebrew; a modern language for calculus; natural history for "intellectual philosophy"; and an ancient or modern language for the chemistry, mineralogy, and geology requirements). But these were the only electives, and all instruction was conducted in recitation form, with students translating, disgorging, or otherwise discoursing on set passages of the assigned text when called upon by the teacher. These recitation sessions—the main form of instruction—lasted from 8 A.M. until noon, and the students' performances were evaluated continuously. They were expected to spend the afternoon hours in study. This rigid, ancient plan of study did teach students to write, to calculate, and to some extent to speak clearly, but it allowed for no concentration in fields of study and little sequential development, excluded students' choices of subjects, and ignored the entire world of modern literature.

Yet students—the best of them, at least—were alive with new intellectual interests, sensitive to new currents of thought and to developing areas of scholarship. Little of this vitality, however, was reflected in the set curriculum. In addition to the *Course of Instruction* described above, the College also published a list of available lectures that had no organic relationship to the set course of study. Professors might insist that students attend, but they could not examine them on the lectures nor assign accompanying reading. Thus in 1824 lectures were announced on divinity and astronomy in the first term; topics in science, medicine, and Hebrew, and on Greek, French, and Spanish literature in the second term; and on science, law, rhetoric, and Greek, French, and Spanish literature in the third term. But no one was obliged to attend any of these lectures, and none were in any way drawn into the preparation for the recitation meetings.

The result of this disjunction between the vital intellectual life of the students and the inherited, rigid curriculum was discontent, cynicism, boredom, and, more constructively, a virtual explosion of private societies in which, however informally and unsystematically, the students explored and expressed their interests. Emerson organized a book club, was secretary of a literary society called the Pythologian, and in his senior year joined the Conventicle, whose officers were called "archbishops" and "bishops." Francis Parkman organized a Chit Chat Club; Thoreau belonged to the Natural History Society, which collected specimens of all sorts on field trips. The old Speakers Club, which sponsored lectures and debates, became a freshman society, and then spawned the Institute of 1770 to do more of the same for the upperclassmen. A Humphrey Davies Society developed the interests of undergraduate chemists. The Society of Christian Brethren was a vehicle of fundamentalists, while the Hasty Pudding and Porcellian Clubs, among others, collected books and maintained private libraries which made a range of reading available that the College library could not, or would not, provide. These clubs embodied the live intellectual interests and ambitions of the undergraduates and hence were vital, informal supplements to the rigid formal curriculum. But they also had the effect of exaggerating by contrast the stodginess of the required course of study and the undergraduates' discontent with it.

This disjunction between the inherited curriculum and the broad intellectual interests of the students tended to magnify a second set of problems, associated with student behavior and discipline. Harvard College in Kirkland's time was deliberately, elaborately, and smotheringly paternalistic. The median age of entering students in 1810 was fifteen and a half, which meant that while some were in their twenties, half were in their early adolescence, and they behaved that way. At the same time, the College maintained unflinchingly its traditional role of proto-parent—and an implacably protective and directive parent it was. It took full and detailed responsibility for the morals and behavior of the students. Tutors (all instructors aside from the professors) were obliged to live in the Yard and to roam the area at night with dark lanterns to see that the students obeyed the parietal rules. The president joined the nightly patrols. But all of this surveillance was dysfunctional if not counterproductive. The atmosphere of Boston in the 1820s was scarcely conducive to Puritan asceticism. While the "immediate government" (the faculty) of the College tightened its rigor to control an increasingly restive population of energetic adolescents and young men, the behavior of the students worsened and became notorious. Attendance in class could be policed, but in the free afternoon hours and in the evenings undergraduates—a few at least, whose numbers increased in the telling—were seen loafing around Boston, smoking, drinking, and whoring. More important, and less speculative, was their behavior on campus. They engaged in almost continuous warfare with the faculty.

Student riots were nothing new at Harvard. There had been serious outbreaks in 1766, in 1769, and in 1805—and they had had no higher justification than disgust at the quality of the food provided in commons or the behavior of certain instructors. They bore no relation to affairs outside of the College, and had no ideological content, academic or otherwise. They were simply explosions of pent-up adolescent energies against the tightly paternalistic, and *increasingly* paternalistic, system.

But they were savage little affairs. A riot in 1818 in which bread was flung through the oriels in the partitions between the common rooms in University Hall continued until most of the College crockery was smashed. Four sophomores were rusticated for this riot, and ex-president Adams (class of 1755) decided that flogging should be revived. On another such occasion, William Prescott, the future historian, was blinded in one eye by a fiercely thrown crust of bread. At one point bonfires suddenly flared up, one of them fueled by the newspapers in the reading room. Gunpowder exploded, pitch barrels were set afire, insulting notes were sent to tutors, attached to cannon balls dropped from the rooftops (one barely missed a wandering professor). In pitched battles between rival student groups, buckets of ink and water were flung about, and occasionally in the classrooms or chapel the voices of unpopular or too longwinded teachers were drowned out by surreptitious foot scrapings on the bare wooden floors. Desperately the tutors tried to keep order, but repeatedly their lives turned into nightmares as they struggled to confine these explosive energies.

All of this was well known to the public, of course, and played into a third disjunction in the life of Kirkland's Harvard. The College had always been a quasi-public institution in the sense that its senior governing board, the Overseers, was drawn from the membership of public bodies, and in the sense that it was supported in part with public funds. This public character was endorsed in the constitution that John Adams wrote for the Commonwealth of Massachusetts in 1780. That instrument of fundamental law included an entire chapter on "The University at Cambridge" in which the Board of Overseers was defined as consisting of the state's governor, lieutenant governor, council and senate, together with the Congregational ministers of Cambridge and five other neighboring towns. The old subsidy continued too. A law of 1814, to expire in 1823, set the amount at $10,000 a year, which was a quarter of the College's operating income.

The continuing connection between Harvard and the state of Massachusetts rested on two underlying conditions. The first was the continuing homogeneity of the state's political population; the second was the continuing vagueness in distinction between public and private functions and agencies. Both, as Kirkland's administration proceeded, were coming under pressure. While the state's population remained predominantly Congregationalist, the College went Unitarian, that is, radical in religion; and at the same time it was conservative (Federalist) in politics, while the state's legislature reflected varying balances between conservatives and liberals or radicals. And further, for reasons rooted in fundamental shifts in the political-legal structure of American life, affecting many spheres of activity, especially business organizations and higher education, the hitherto vague distinction between things "public" and things "private" was becoming sharper. Long before Kirkland's time Harvard's public subsidy had come under attack, and only an exceptionally secure control of the legislature by Federalists in 1814 made the annual grants of Kirkland's first decade possible.

Harvard's traditional if limited role as a public agency was seriously questioned by a political population that admired neither its politics nor its manners and that resented its state subsidy. Student riots seemed to exemplify everything wrong with the College, which on top of all else was seen by many as elitist, snobbish, and undoubtedly debauched.

Such were the problems that were emerging systematically and dangerously from the extension of traditional forms into a new and different world—a grotesquely dysfunctional curriculum; student behavior that violated the paternalistic assumptions of both the College and the public at large; and a continuing public character increasingly anomalous in a society in which the distinction between public and private spheres was growing steadily sharper in law and in practice. Kirkland's popularity continued unabated, but the institution as a whole was increasingly vulnerable. A crisis can now be seen to have been almost inevitable. Any severe jolt would have led to a general upheaval which would have forced all of these problems into the open and precipitated solutions of one kind or another—good, bad, or indifferent. The jolt came in 1823 in the form of one of the worst student riots in Harvard's history.

The class of 1823 was exceptionally wild. As sophomores they too had broken the crockery in University Hall and then had proceeded to destroy doors and windows in the building. When three students had been suspended, general rioting ensued, and there were demonstrations in the chapel. The climax came two years later. In May 1823 rivalry between two students for Commencement roles led to unfounded charges of corruption against one and the ostracism of the other. When the Faculty intervened and punished the accused, his partisans conspired to retaliate against the accuser, which they did by hissing his performance on Exhibition Day and turning the chapel into an uproar. When the original victim was dismissed, wrongly, for organizing this protest, his friends resolved that they would never attend another College exercise if their enemy participated. And so when the villain boldly appeared in chapel in University Hall the conspirators created an immense uproar, and then picked him up bodily and threw him down the stairs. For this, four students were expelled, and when the rest repeated the tactic on the next occasion and promised to treat their enemy to more of the same in the future, and in addition to "*thrash* him severely" if he ever showed his face again, thirty-seven members of the senior class were dismissed from the College.

The list included some of the most distinguished names in Massachusetts, and elsewhere: Adams, Amory, Carroll (of Maryland), Choate, Coolidge, Crowninshield, Dunbar (of Natchez), Inches, Loring, Peabody, Pickering, Sturgis, Sumner. In all, forty-three members of the senior class were dismissed in the course of these disturbances a month before their Commencement, and the families concerned rose up in arms. The most eloquent letter was written from Washington by the Secretary of State, John Quincy Adams (class of 1787) then in the midst of developing the Monroe Doctrine. Indeed, one wonders which problem occupied him more in May 1823, the defense of the Western Hemisphere from the ambitions of the European powers or the reinstatement of his dismissed son John. His main letter to Kirkland (he apparently wrote several) is a major effort of statesmanship, rhetoric, and ingenious reasoning. The Secretary of State assured President Kirkland that he was well aware of the need to maintain law and order, and he also assured him of his endless affection for his alma mater. But he demanded to know if some other mode of punishment than dismissal could not be found. Dismissal, he said, was a punishment appropriate to an individual, not to "the aggregate transgressions of nearly a whole class." The postponement of the honor of the degree was indeed a disgrace, degrading an individual in the opinion of the country, and so it was a severe punishment for two or three individuals without injuring the institution itself. "But a *degraded Class!*—Would it not necessarily shed some of its dishonour upon the University itself?" Two centuries of Harvard's history had unrolled, and while there had been many riots, "never yet had it exhibited to the contempt of the world, the example of a *degraded Class.*" Furthermore, punishment meted out to forty-three of the class of seventy would dishonor the reputation of the innocent. But it was the dishonor to Harvard that he mainly stressed: "I ask again, will it not be the dishonour of the University and of the Commonwealth? A dishonour, the more Shameful as it will befall bodies legally immortal; while that of the degraded individuals will at least be washed away by death."

This lofty appeal—which concluded with the charge, "Save the honour of our native State"—was unavailing. Kirkland and the faculty stood firm, and were backed by the Corporation. At least fourteen of the forty-three dismissed seniors never received degrees. The rest were awarded theirs at various times in the 1840s and '50s—all except one individual whose degree was delayed for 57 years, and John Adams, whose degree was finally awarded in 1873, thirty-nine years after his death.

The great rebellion of 1823 and its conclusion in the expulsion of over half of the senior class created an immense furor, quite aside from the reactions of the families directly affected. It brought to the surface all of the problems that had been latently developing, stirred up all of the discontents that until then had been contained by Kirkland's paternalistic care and amiability, and revealed the limits of the president's effectiveness in attempting to deal with new and difficult issues by the graceful deployment of traditional means. The issues that suddenly erupted were explosive, profound, and they were compounded by two chronological coincidences which further contributed to the turmoil that followed the May days of 1823.

The first was the death of a member of the Corporation a few weeks after the rebellion, and the resulting necessity to fill the vacancy. Led by two of the College's most distinguished scholars, Andrews Norton, Dexter Lecturer on Biblical Literature, and the young German-trained Edward Everett, the first Eliot Professor of Greek

Literature, both men of exceptionally healthy egos, a group of the faculty attempted to fill the seat with one of their own immediate colleagues. More than that, they renewed and elaborated all the old arguments, presumably laid to rest a century earlier, to the effect that the resident faculty *was*, or if it wasn't it should be, the Corporation itself, and that a separate board external to the resident faculty violated the terms of the University's charter. The arguments, in essence long familiar, had never been presented so elaborately and cogently as they were in the faculty's Memorial to the Corporation of April 1824, supported by a brace of appended documents. The Corporation referred the matter to the Overseers, and the faculty petitioners then trained their guns on that body, arguing that "by the charter of the University, the Fellows of the University are required to be resident instructors." The duel was begun, and this time it was fought to the finish.

While the Overseers were pondering their response, one of their number, John Lowell, fired off a pamphlet denying all of the faculty's claims, and denying too the idea that the faculty would be any better off if the Corporation were filled with their members. Everett, never at a loss for words or arguments, replied at once, provoking still another set of arguments from Lowell. In the midst of all this, George Ticknor, the newly appointed Smith Professor of the French and Spanish Languages and of Belles-lettres, who agreed with Everett in questions of academic reform, entered the scene. He delivered an extraordinarily cogent, learned, and sensible attack on the faculty's position, based especially on what he claimed was a misunderstanding on the faculty's part of the origins and present state of collegiate corporations in the English universities. The Fellows of English colleges had *not* always been, and were not now, all teachers; some individuals had in fact been paid by corporate funds *not* to teach. And they had not been, and were not now, all residents in the colleges. What their fellowships had required them to do, what they had been and were being paid to do, was to *learn*, to develop their scholarship to the highest degree possible, something, he wrote pointedly, that no one had ever accused the Harvard faculty of doing.

In the end, the Overseers, adding their own detailed and carefully argued gloss to the publications that had already appeared, voted unanimously against the faculty's position, and they set out three resolutions which settled the matter once and for all. First, they said, the resident instructors have no exclusive right to be chosen Fellows of the Corporation; second, Fellows of the Corporation do not forfeit their seats by not residing in the College; and third, future elections to the Corporation need follow no set prescription.

The debate had been intense, public, and argued by people who knew a remarkable amount about the English practice which Harvard's was supposed to have followed. The legal points might well have remained arguable—despite the fact that the Board of Overseers included some of the Commonwealth's most distinguished lawyers and jurists. But the practical point made by the Overseers proved persuasive, namely, that the faculty as the Corporation could become an irresponsible body, since it would be charged with almost unlimited power to supervise and regulate itself. "Such a body of men," Ticknor wrote, "would hardly fail, in the course of a few generations, to make a College, as much and as truly a monopoly for their own benefit, as anything in the English universities."

So the accident of the death of a member of the Corporation precipitated a two-year struggle between members of the faculty and the governing boards about the fundamental character of Harvard as an institution, a struggle whose origins reached back to the early seventeenth century. The implications for the whole of American higher education, as Ticknor explained in his exhaustive and closely reasoned pamphlet, were profound. But in a deeper sense the timing of the explosion was no accident. The faculty was restive, frustrated, and in part infused with new ideas and new ambitions. Sooner or later the question of the extent of its authority would have to emerge; the sudden vacancy simply provided the occasion.

Another seeming accident also precipitated a definitive solution to another profound question. The legislative subsidy to Harvard and to the two other Masssachusetts colleges (Williams and Bowdoin) had been passed in 1814 for a period of ten years, which meant that it came up for renewal in the same year, 1823, in which so much else was happening—indeed, the matter came to a head during the weeks of the riot and its immediate aftermath. And coupled with this question was a proposal to charter Amherst College, "to check the progress of errors which are propagated from Cambridge." A Federalist, latitudinarian legislature was likely to defeat the Amherst campaign, and so every effort was made by the conservatives to elect Republicans to the General Court and to condemn Harvard for its infidelity, its licentiousness, and general corruption. The Rebellion was a wonderful boon to that campaign. The legislature went Republican in the fall of 1823. Amherst received its charter, and Harvard, and Williams along with it, lost its state subsidy. The College would never again receive financial support from the state of Massachusetts, and to that extent it became, in 1823, much more than it ever had been before, a "private" institution, though the presence of state officials on the Board of Overseers—53 members out of a total of 84 in Kirkland's time—continued to represent what Ticknor called "the public interest in the institution."

In neither of these two major developments in the tumultuous year of change, 1823—the definitive settlement of the nature of the Corporation and the permanent removal of public funds from Harvard—did Kirkland play a significant role. Perhaps no one in his position could have had an effect in either case. The sole member of both faculty and Corporation, Kirkland could only suffer by supporting one side or another; and advocacy of public support could only have alienated further the Republican religious-conservative coalition. But in the chief issue of the time, the central struggle precipitated by the Rebellion, his leadership was sorely needed, and it was not forthcoming.

The faculty reformers had every reason to expect Kirkland's active support, if not leadership, in their effort to revamp the curriculum, recast the forms of instruction, sophisticate the disciplinary system, and transform the College into a university-level center of scholarship. For Kirkland himself had set the process in motion when, in 1815, he had appointed to the new Eliot Professorship of Greek Literature the 21-year-old Edward Everett. The precocious Unitarian minister was as brilliant then, and as egotistical, though perhaps not yet as ineffective, as he would later be as congressman, governor, minister to Britain, Harvard president, Secretary of State, and Gettysburg orator. At twenty-one, the man whom Emerson would later describe as "a mere dangler and ornamental person," had had all the promise in the world, and the Corporation, at Kirkland's bidding, had made the extraordinary decision to pay his salary in full for two years while he traveled abroad to advance his learning and broaden his view of the world. It was Kirkland too who had first recognized the ability of Everett's three traveling companions in Europe: George Ticknor, whom he had appointed at the age of twenty-five, when he was still in Europe, to the new Smith Professorship of the French and Spanish Languages and of Belles-lettres; George Bancroft, the future historian, whom he had supported in Europe on some kind of personal fellowship and then appointed Tutor in Greek; and Joseph Cogswell, whom he had appointed College Librarian and Professor of Mineralogy and Geology.

The European odyssey of this famous quadrumvirate—their stay in Göttingen and their discovery of central European scholarship and university life, their fascination with true erudition and the demands it made on intellect and character, their meetings with Goethe in Weimar, with Benjamin Constant, Madame De Staël, and Alexander von Humboldt in Paris, with Byron in Venice, with Sir Walter Scott in Scotland, with Bunsen and the Bonaparte circle in Rome, and with the marvels of Greece—this wonderful story of Yankees abroad, moving with superb *panache* from the American periphery of Western culture into its inner, most creative core, has often been told and need not be retold here. By 1822 all four were installed at Harvard, all four were appalled at the crabbed provincialism and childish educational system they found in the College, all four were determined to transform the system if they could, and all four were convinced they had Kirkland's support in making the effort.

In the end they all failed, and withdrew from the fray, though at different times and in different ways. Bancroft, unsuccessful in a personal effort to divide his Greek sections by proficiency, quit Harvard and the "sickening and wearisome" Cambridge after a single year, and joined Cogswell in founding the progressive Roundhill School at Northampton, Massachusetts. Both felt that Kirkland had failed to provide the support he had promised and which they needed to make a significant dent in the old text-and-recitation system. Everett lasted longer—five years, before he took off for greater personal rewards in politics. But he at least, in his lectures, managed to convey to susceptible undergraduates like Emerson something of the excitement of true German scholarship, something of the intellectual sophistication he had encountered abroad, and something of the personal dignity of the accomplished men of letters he had met on his travels. His impact on

33

the Harvard community during his short tenure was enormous—"the rudest undergraduate," Emerson wrote, "found a new morning opened to him in the lecture-room of Harvard Hall"—but it was ephemeral. Everett had better things to do than to continue the battle with Harvard's entrenched educational system.

So it was left for Ticknor alone to persist in the campaign of reform, and this he did to the best of his ability. His effectiveness was somewhat limited at the start by a superior manner, a snobbishness both social and intellectual, which made it difficult for him to lead his easily intimidated faculty colleagues. The distance between him and the ruck of the harassed teachers took manifest form in his residence in Boston, rather than in the Yard. There, he became the center of a celebrated circle of *erudits*, intellectuals, and fanciers of the arts. But he was serious and persistent in his scholarship, and at the College began an innovative course of lectures on French and Spanish literature, lectures which would later be seen to have anticipated his crowning achievement, the three-volume *History of Spanish Literature*. But however successful his lectures were in intellectual terms, pedagogically they remained anomalous. They simply perched ornamentally atop a hierarchy of recitation classes, and had nothing to do with that basic educational process. The regular, daily education the students received in no way prepared them to appreciate lectures like Ticknor's, nor did his lectures assist the students in conquering the daily quotas of book learning assigned for recitation.

By 1821 Ticknor was using his influence with the members of the governing boards at least to survey faculty opinion on fundamental reform. But the results were discouraging. His hopes were fading and his pedagogical ambitions were flagging when the Rebellion of 1823 transformed the situation. Everyone was suddenly convinced that something was basically wrong with the system, and that fundamental changes were in order. Ticknor, together with a few of the more erudite, ambitious, and well-connected members of the faculty, joined with several Overseers immediately after the Rebellion to force the process of reform forward. The result was the production of a small shelf of studies and reports submitted by a tangle of interlocked committees—reports of the Overseers; reports of the Corporation; reports of the two boards together; reports of the faculty; and comments on each report by the authors of the others. In this blizzard of paper that blew up in Cambridge between July 1823 and June 1825, when the revised "Statutes and Laws of the University in Cambridge, Massachusetts" was agreed on, one document stands out: the report of the Overseers' Committee to Investigate the College, chaired by Joseph Story (class of 1798), associate justice of the United States Supreme Court. A relatively short document, submitted in May 1824, it cut to the heart of the unresolved problems that were beset-ting Kirkland's Harvard; and it discussed lucidly some of the most persistent and deep-lying problems facing all would-be reformers of higher education, then and later.

It is true, Story's committee wrote, that Harvard was flourishing. Its reputation as the nation's leading university had never been higher. In the previous twenty years it had undergone various changes as professorships had multiplied and new forms of instruction and new bodies of knowledge had been introduced. But these changes, the committee pointed out, had been "engrafted upon the existing sys-tem, from time to time, without that system itself having undergone a general and correspondent modification." American society was al-ways changing, and always would change, and "the nature and extent of an University education, and the methods of instruction, must be, in some degree, liable to change, so as to be adopted to the spirit of the age. A course of studies, fully adequate at one period, to all the wants and wishes of the community, may be ill fitted for another of higher cultivation. . . . A system is not therefore necessarily good for the future, because it has accomplished much good in the past." The community at large in the current age, the committee believed, de-manded "a more thorough education and higher attainments . . . both for active and professional life" than had been offered before. "A more efficient system" of instruction and discipline was now needed to "gratify the publick wants, and increase the usefulness of collegiate studies."

First, the committee said, the internal administration of the Col-lege must be revamped. Specifically, the president should be relieved of those everyday administrative duties that derived from a simpler era and which at present occupied so much of his time. He should be provided with a secretary and should concentrate on general policy matters and "a general superintendence" of all of the College's con-cerns. He should have scrutiny of the work of every branch of the

College, and should report to the Corporation regularly, in writing. At the same time, teaching should be organized into subject matter departments, each headed by a professor and staffed by tutors and instructors. And under the professor's supervision, instruction should be shifted away from the digestion of set texts to the study of whole subjects. Further, discipline should be reordered, and responsibility placed in the hands of an administrative committee for each residential building, chaired by a professor, the chairmen together constituting a College-wide administrative board whose recommendations could be effected only by the president. Third, studies should be divided into two groups: College-wide basic requirements, "indispensable to obtain a degree," and studies undergraduates themselves selected. Recitation should continue, but in much smaller groups, much more searchingly conducted, and with opportunity for "familiar teaching and inquiries by verbal explanations and criticisms of the Instructer." Notes were to be taken at lectures, and professors were to examine students on the subjects of the lectures as part of a greatly reinforced annual examination system. Fourth, "the demands of our country for scientifick knowledge" had become such that students should be admitted who were not degree candidates. Such graduate, or non-degree students, should be allowed to pick their subjects with complete freedom and be awarded certificates for successful completion of their work. Fifth, vacations should be shortened—ten weeks per calendar year was quite enough—and absences in term time should be strictly controlled. Sixth, the old system of punishment by fines, which largely fell on parents, should be abolished, and "tasks, or some other equivalents, which shall operate directly on the students themselves, be substituted in their stead." Students' behavior should be closely examined; every student's room should be visited by a College officer at 9 o'clock every evening, and exhaustive reports on students' behavior and accomplishments should be submitted to the students' parents every quarter. And, to minimize the problem of discipline, the committee recommended sixteen as the minimum age of entrance.

Finally, the cost of an education at Harvard should be reduced as far as possible, so that families "of moderate property, and in the middle rank of life, may not be deterred from sending their children to Cambridge, nor obliged to seek a cheaper or more defective education elsewhere." To this end sumptuary laws should be devised. All

Memorial Hall: The rush for breakfast.

students should be required to eat in commons where "simple and nutritious" meals should be served; servants should be eliminated from the residential buildings; "a uniform dress, more distinct and marked and cheaper than the present, [should] be adopted, to be worn by all the students; and . . . a badge be appropriated for each class, which shall at once strike the eye of an observer." To protect parents against escalating costs for the College uniforms, all such clothing should be made by College workmen, furnished by the College steward, and charged the parents on term bills. Further to cut costs, wherever possible professorships should be allowed to remain unfilled, and the funds thus released be used to reduce the level of tuition.

These were the substantive recommendations of the Story committee of 1823–24. It concluded with two general, procedural considerations. The committee recommended that the changes be put into effect promptly, but not in situations where to do so would violate the rights of professors "under the present statutes of their foundations"—where, in other words, the original rights, "real or imaginary," of professorial appointments would be violated. Where such a danger existed, the assent of the affected professors should be obtained. For the future, however, no appointments should be made without the appointees' consenting to the new conditions. And at the very end, the committee turned, with great vigor, to the question of Harvard's character as a public institution. Its words on this sensitive issue, anachronistic when written, reflect an urgent need to retain an ancient tradition under altered conditions. The Commonwealth of Massachusetts, that is to say the Great and General Court, the Committee wrote, was the original founder and patron of Harvard College, and it still has "a deep interest in its prosperity." From Harvard's point of view, the future patronage of the state was "both desirable and important to its support."

> Whatever, therefore, can have an effect in making the Government of the State more intimately acquainted with its wants and its services, its science and its finances, its pursuits and its objects, will essentially contribute to secure for it a deep publick interest, disarm unfounded prejudices, and conciliate publick favour.

To reinforce Harvard's connection with the General Court and thus to reinforce its public character, the committee recommended that the Board of Overseers meet in the State Senate chamber; that the president, the treasurer, and the several professors should present their annual reports at those open meetings; and that the Boston newspapers should carry notice of the meetings ten days in advance to enable the interested public to attend.

Such was the notable report of Story's committee of the Board of Overseers, a trenchant and perceptive account of Harvard's deficiencies and of the need for constant scrutiny in the face of inevitable change. Its recommendations were for the most part imaginative, shaped by a sense of Harvard's great potentiality to become an advanced university college. Much influenced by the views of Ticknor, Everett, Norton, and the other sophisticates on the Harvard faculty, it yet attempted to retain essential features of the old College. Its recommendations not only reinvoked but strengthened and elaborated the College's role as pseudo-parent. The right of the existing faculty to resist change if their real interests were involved was flatly defended. The committee also refused to pronounce on the critical issue of whether or not students should be grouped by proficiency and level of knowledge and be urged to advance as quickly as they could, that being, the committee said, too controversial a question for them to decide. And the committee boldly reasserted Harvard's identity as a public institution, its welfare a matter of public concern. Harvard's goals, it said, should not be defined by the narrow academic interests and satisfactions of its faculty but should be devoted "to the spirit of the age," "to the present exigencies of our society, so as to give the most finished education . . . that our pursuits require." The College should respond to what is "demanded by the community at large, both for active and professional life." Everything the committee wrote was infused with the belief "that a more efficient system can be put into operation, to gratify the publick wants, and increase the usefulness of collegiate studies."

After much discussion, Story's report was endorsed by the Overseers and sent to the Corporation for implementation. The result was the revised "Statutes and Laws of the University in Cambridge, Massachusetts" (1825). A document of 153 laws in 13 chapters, the new code was both more and less than Story's committee and the Ticknor group behind it had hoped for. It changed the vacation schedule, redefined the president's role and his formal responsibility to the governing boards, abolished fines as punishment, and organized a stricter system of supervising students' behavior, though it did not create the recommended system of administrative committees. More important, it organized the faculty into departments for the first time, and in the controversial and completely revolutionary law 61, went beyond Story's proposals and divided students into classes by "their proficiency and capacity, and each division shall be encouraged as rapidly as may be found consistent with a thorough knowledge of the subjects of their studies."

In all of this—the furnishing of ideas to Story's committee, the debate on the Report the committee submitted, and the implementation by the Corporation—Kirkland played an ambiguous and largely silent role. As the original sponsor and patron of Ticknor and the other advanced members of the faculty, he implicitly favored their interests; as the popular embodiment of the old regime at its genial best, he appeared to favor the inertia and traditionalism of the majority of the faculty, which had no desire to transform the system and saw only marginal roles for themselves in the new world that Ticknor sought. So the president largely fell silent, disappointing both sides, the reformers by failing to advance their cause, the traditionalists by failing to oppose change and by having sponsored the revolutionaries in the first place.

It was perhaps to goad Kirkland into action, and certainly to relieve himself of his own frustrations and concerns for the future, that Ticknor published in 1825, as the new laws were about to go into effect, his *Remarks on Changes Lately Proposed or Adopted in Harvard University*. More than four times longer than Story's report, written with passion and a compulsive exhaustiveness and concern for detail, the pamphlet reviewed all the main issues. Ticknor condemned the "authorized idleness" of the students, the "nugatory show" of the examination system, the stupidity of the disciplinary system, and above all the antiquated instructional system. He approved and enthusiastically endorsed most of Story's recommendations, but regretted that they did not go far enough. Studies should be *entirely* elective, and grouping by proficiency—"the broad corner stone for beneficial changes in all our colleges" and the best way to advance learning and keep down "extensive combinations or rebellions"—should be carried out to the fullest possible extent. Examinations should be totally revamped and tightened up. Above all, "the principle of thorough TEACHING" should be the foundation, the "cynosure," of all the changes undertaken. Good teaching should involve "thorough commentary" on the topics treated, as well as explanation and illustration by the teachers at every stage, for "young men may be *taught* as well as examined." Only then could they be properly educated and Harvard's and all the other colleges' facilities be put to proper use.

By the time Ticknor's pamphlet appeared, the new code was in process of implementation, a process that moved forward under the immediate supervision of the president. As the plans began to be realized, Ticknor's disappointment and dissatisfaction grew. The majority of the faculty, it had long been clear, had little interest in the key change, the grouping of the classes by proficiency; and the parents, who saw it as a strange kind of intellectual elitism altogether improper in a democracy, were even more opposed. Both the faculty and the parents considered the new system unfair to the average or below average student. The more the real meaning of the change became clear, the more Kirkland drifted away from Ticknor, whose persistence he began to find annoying, and the more he found his sympathies drawn to the opposition. Increasingly, he ignored Ticknor's pleas, neglected even to inform him how his lectures were to be organized and whether or not modern languages would constitute one of the new departments. When in January 1826 law 61 went into effect, many of the faculty dragged their feet and in some cases deliberately defied the new system. By the end of the term, Kirkland had fallen entirely into the opposition, and in November he led through the Corporation a modification of the law, which made its implementation optional by department. By January 1827 all departments except Ticknor's had abandoned the new system, though there, in the department of modern languages, it continued on, to the great benefit of all students of French and Spanish Languages and Literatures, subjects which quickly became the most popular in the College.

In these years of controversy and change, 1823–1827, Kirkland's image was tarnished. Still popular, still seen as a genial embodiment of a comfortable but clearly antiquated educational system, he had failed to bridge the old world and the new. Leadership had fallen to others, and while he had not, at first, resisted change, neither had he shaped it, nor had he drawn his faculty into it to any significant degree. He had largely stood aside, letting his avant garde proteges and their allies on the governing boards take the initiative while the majority of the faculty dug in their heels and appealed to him for support. At no time did he fully understand or, if he understood, did he act on, the profound assumption of Story's committee that only confusion and frustration would result from a situation in which changes were merely "engrafted upon the existing system, from time to time, without that system itself [undergoing] a general and correspondent modification." It was left for another president, a generation later, to define and implement the comprehensive restructuring that Ticknor had sought and that Kirkland had never fully comprehended.

But by the spring of 1827 curricular reform was no longer the only, or even the most urgent, major problem facing Kirkland. In 1825–26 the composition of the Corporation was altered by four vacancies and replacements. Among the new members was Dr. Nathaniel Bowditch, mathematician and scientist, famous author of *The Practical Navigator*, and a meticulous bookkeeper and administrative precisionist. As a long-standing former member of the Board of Overseers, he was well aware of Kirkland's popularity and of his administrative informality as well. Both respectful of and somewhat baffled by the president's bland and cheerful manner, he was determined to straighten out what he took to be the administrative confusion that reigned. He tangled with Kirkland immediately, first on marginal matters and then, savagely, on basic fiscal questions. As chairman of the Corporation's finance committee, he discovered that the Treasurer under Kirkland, John Davis, had reduced the College's accounts to chaos and was responsible for large errors in bookkeeping. The results of Kirkland's personal informality were even more glaring, and to Bowditch no less irresponsible. For years, Kirkland had ignored his regular salary and simply drawn on the steward when he needed money; in the end he was overdrawn by $1700. He gave worthy and needy students financial assistance when he thought they required it, consulting no one and using for this purpose not only currently available cash but also $1000 of the College's capital. Further, the new professorial chairs which he had filled so imaginatively and ambitiously had been underendowed, and salaries had been paid only by juggling the funds around in strange and unseemly ways. And the College's rents had been neglected, its timber properties in Maine left to trespassers, its securities mislaid, and what appeared to Bowditch to be extravagances in expenditures allowed to continue.

Having uncovered these conditions, Bowditch went to work. Under his leadership, salaries (including the president's) were cut, non-resident teachers were fired, teaching assignments were increased and reduced to strict schedules, charity to students was regularized, the accounts brought under strict control, excessive expenditures eliminated, and Kirkland's minor laxity forced back into line. Kirkland could no longer ignore the Corporation's orders when he disliked them, and indeed could no longer preside effectively over the College in the way he had, with so much success, for seventeen years. In August 1827 he had a slight stroke, and though by October he had recovered sufficiently to resume his duties, and indeed in September had married for the first time, his effectiveness as president had clearly been destroyed. Bowditch could see the end, and in February 1828 seized on a minor matter, in which Kirkland seemed to be resisting the Corporation's order to clear a suite of rooms in Hollis for Ticknor's use as classrooms, to attack the president directly. In a blistering tirade, he accused Kirkland of trying to thwart the Corporation's efforts at retrenchment and of having neglected to make the improvements he was supposed to have made. Whether or not in the fateful Corporation meeting Bowditch called Kirkland an "imbecile," as he was later accused of having done, history does not record. But he certainly abused him severely, and the next day, March 28, 1828, Kirkland resigned.

The testimonies to Kirkland that followed were sincere. The Corporation recognized the "singular dignity and mildness" with which he had presided, "his splendid talents and accomplishments, his paternal care, and his faithful services." The Overseers too recognized his accomplishments. But it is the students' address to the former president that properly reflects the affection in which he had been held. In a touching testimonial written by members of the senior class, they condemned the "malignity" with which his physical weakness had been taken advantage of, the way he had been worn down "with petty calumnies" and had suddenly been censured for "inadvertent errors or improvident virtues." Such mistreatment was to be denounced by all just men, they wrote. For themselves, the students chose to recall "the multitude of good works and words, we have received at your hand."

> We thank you, sir, imperfectly, but heartily. We thank you for the honors which your award has made more sweet, and we thank you for the reproof which has been tempered with love. We thank you for the benignity of manners which engaged our confidence, for the charities which secured our hearts. We thank you, sir, for all the little, nameless, unremembered acts of your kindness and authority. We are deeply in your debt, but the obligation is not irksome; it is a debt of gratitude we are well pleased to owe.

No more moving tribute has ever been paid to a Harvard president, and none has been better deserved. Kirkland's failure—if it can be called that; he was eminently successful for over a decade—was a product of historical change he could not control. His relaxed geniality and encouragement of a sophisticated literary style was a breath of fresh air in the antiquated eighteenth-century institution he had inherited, and he encouraged the most advanced spirits among the intellectually ambitious young men he encountered. He stimulated advancement, growth, and sophistication, but he did not see the ways in which the developments he was encouraging conflicted with the fundamentals of the system he had inherited and the style that was so natural and enjoyable to him. Never an "administrator" in a modern sense, and never a systematic thinker, he did not recognize the confusion that resulted from the accumulation of *ad hoc* changes "without that system itself," in Story's words, "having undergone a general and correspondent modification." So, immensely popular, immensely attractive, and immensely supportive to the enterprising spirits of the age, he helped bring into being a situation full of anomalies and ambiguities. By the early 1820s, the paradoxes had become blatant, the situation confusing beyond easy clarification. The system, fragile in its inner contradictions, was held together mainly by the president's attractive presence. When a single, powerful blow destroyed the College's equanimity and set in motion reforms aimed at thoroughgoing clarification and systematization, Kirkland was caught in the middle. Neither a revolutionary nor a reactionary, recognizing the values of the new world of learning but incapable of directing it and unwilling to see it destroy the ambience in which he had flourished, he fell silent, and slowly drifted backward into support of the faculty's inertia. Nothing illustrates so vividly the complexities of Harvard's painful passage into modernity as the failure of its most popular president to comprehend it.

Class Day in Harvard Yard, 1895.

OSCAR HANDLIN

Making Men
of the Boys

For the first two centuries and a half Harvard's history unfolded according to a pattern of classic elegance—its noble theme, the unexpected fruit of the beneficent spread of liberty. In the beginning the College was unformed and darkness was upon the face of the Yard. With the Revolution came Enlightenment, which led to the flowering of the nineteenth century and, under the guidance of Charles W. Eliot (class of 1853), to the mature fruit of the twentieth century. The epic is not only edifying; it also true—mostly. It obscures, however, aspects of the story less neatly told, as well as persistent inner contradictions that paradoxically accounted for both the achievements and the failures of the institution.

Much changed in 350 years. But one relationship did not—that between those who wielded authority and those subject to it—and the tensions inherent in that relationship explained much in Harvard's development. Adversary is too strong an adjective to apply to the relationship of teachers and pupils; intermittent conflict is the more appropriate term.

Authority from the beginning rested in the hands of the President and Fellows of Harvard College. Although the Board of Overseers possessed a general supervisory mandate, the Corporation was the ruling body, endowed with plenary power to govern the institution and to manage its property. It provided formal continuity, enacted the statutes, made appointments, and awarded degrees. But unless a crisis intervened, the day-to-day, year-to-year, conduct of education fell to the lot of the president, who resided in the College, often taught, and presided over both governing boards. From Henry Dunster who took office in 1640 to Abbott Lawrence Lowell (class of 1877) who accepted the post in 1909, the president was the dominant figure in the University. Up to a point! Few in that long succession from Dunster onward enjoyed happy or even tolerable administrations. Edward Holyoke (class of 1705) was more fortunate than most. He served thirty-two years and died at the age of eighty. At the affecting deathbed scene, the mourners who hung upon his valedictory words heard him sigh, "If any man wishes to be humbled and mortified, let him become President of Harvard College."

However clear the authority of the Corporation, another, less formal, force also operated in Cambridge. Those subject to authority, usually flaccid and acquiescent, on occasion mounted such resistance as could shatter a president. Harvard education was not simply the product of the will of the governing boards and teachers; the victims of their ministrations imposed their own necessities on the system. In that respect the classes of 1700, 1800, and 1900 were remarkably similar. In all three centuries the character of the student body and the motives for the students' enrollment profoundly influenced the institution.

The founders of the College were clear in their own minds about its function. Soon after they had provided for their livelihood, for God's worship, and for civil government, the next thing they longed for and looked after was to advance learning and perpetuate it to posterity, dreading to leave an illiterate ministry to the churches when their present ministers died. Dedication to learning indeed endured in the centuries that followed. In that respect Harvard continued the tradition of the English universities from which it descended.

But neither in the Old World nor the New did colleges expect to recruit only prospective divines as students. A significant number of graduates did go on to careers in the church, but not all; fewer than half did in the seventeenth century and, before long, the percentage of alumni in other callings steadily increased. Congregationalism and its offshoots were not the growth denominations of the nineteenth and twentieth centuries. Harvard, like other colleges, was therefore willing—nay eager—to enroll students who had no intention of entering the ministry.

The correspondence of Governor John Winthrop with Mrs. Emmanuel Downing (1636–1637) hinted at another function. The Governor suggested that the new seminary would also furnish an alternative for parents in England who viewed with distaste the corruption of Oxford and Cambridge. Their children—her son George—would breathe a purer atmosphere in the New World. While it was not true that the desire to provide for the Downing scion (class of 1642) prompted the foundation of the College, it was true that then and later a market existed for a pious atmosphere in which lads could learn a little logic, Greek, Hebrew, or the like while they passed through the difficult years of transition to manhood. Harvard aimed to provide that atmosphere as did the English universities. Far back in the thirteenth century, when Walter de Merton had founded a college in Oxford, he did so to strengthen the knowledge of letters but also because he had a number of nephews unprovided for.

The happy intersection of two sets of motives combined to raise the number of students at Harvard. Periods of stagnation and even of decline did not long interrupt the process of growth, but, alas, there was little evidence that the increase reflected a widening concern with learning among the country's young people. Parents had their own reasons for sending away their children and Harvard had a cause of its own for welcoming them. The teachers and the students, the parties most directly affected, had somewhat different views of the matter but their voices counted for little in these decisions.

The presidents of the College generally welcomed and the faculty usually deplored growth. To those who taught them, the pupils never seemed well enough prepared. To Professor Levi Hedge (class of 1792), the entering class of 1806 appeared "to be a huge body, composed of heterogeneous materials, some of which are not more than half seasoned, some sappy, corky and worm-eaten. One would suppose all the minor seminaries had disgorged their contents good and bad, and we had them en masse." The huge body to which he referred numbered seventy-five; and would increase steadily later in the century. Hedge blamed the growth, as professors would persist in doing, on lax examinations and lowered standards. And he was correct. Nevertheless the presidents continued to welcome growth. Abstract standards were less important than the income needed to pay the bills. The truth was that until well into the twentieth century the tuition payer was welcome, at any age. Those who could not meet all the formal admissions requirements could enter with conditions as special students. The main objective was to sustain cash flow.

Harvard was always poor, strapped by a meager endowment. Income from that source averaged £156 a year between 1693 and 1712. In its first century and a half the funds available to it grew at a pitiful rate, and by the time of the Revolution they had scarcely increased. Furthermore, the colonial economy afforded no opportunities for endowment to produce substantial income. Neither loans at interest, nor annuities, nor land—the only means of investment— were dependable. In any case, mismanagement by Treasurer John Hancock (class of 1754) and the disturbances of war wiped away practically the whole College stock. In the nineteenth century, despite Harvard's longevity, prestige, and reputation, the total remained small and vulnerable to inflation, less than $200,000 in 1845. Lotteries and government grants rarely helped for long. In the end the University depended heavily on fees from tuition so that its income fluctuated with the ups and downs of registration.

The precarious condition endured on into the twentieth century. The thin margin of survival emerged inadvertently in President Eliot's report of 1903–1904. Decades of reform, growth, and precariously achieved stability had not eased the straitened state of University resources. Deploring the budgetary deficits of seven out of the preceding nine years, Eliot explained how dependent Harvard was on income from students. In the spring he had worked hard to cut the salary list of the Faculty of Arts and Sciences by $25,000 in order to balance the budget. But in October of the same year when registration was complete, he discovered that the loss of 118 students, on whose presence (and fees) he had depended, had cut University income by $23,000 and hence left him another deficit. Faced with uncertainty from year to year, the administration was always eager for customers, whether destined for the ministry or not. In addition, the fact was that aspiring clergymen and their parents were not likely to afford the fees that would assure solvency.

In the early years as in the later, the University depended on attracting the sons of men with means, who could pay the necessary tuition. Fortunately, enough parents had reasons of their own to fill the ranks with their offspring. They rarely responded to the waves of rhetoric that accompanied discussions of the value of higher education. Preachers and orators did not lack for familiar phrases trotted out to inveigle support from the legislature or to persuade the surrounding community that the College was beneficial, because it conveyed ideas of virtue to future citizens and trained learned magistrates. Its graduates were "ornaments to society and blessings to their country." Those who uttered these commonplaces sincerely believed them. But these were hardly the reasons why fathers paid their sons' fees.

Nor, down to the end of the nineteenth century, did the desire to ready a lad for a career enter into the decision to send him to Harvard. Higher education was not a preparation for, or even an advantage in, securing access to any of the desirable American callings. College was not a necessary stage on the road to riches—not even in Massachusetts or New England, certainly not elsewhere in the country. Francis Cabot Lowell (class of 1793) did stick it out, but he was the son of a Fellow of the Corporation and the grandson of a minister. On the other hand George Cabot of Salem came to Cambridge in 1766 at the age of fourteen, drudged away at books for a while, took offense at the stinking butter served in commons and then left. He decided to get on with the world's work at sea and by the age of eighteen captained his own vessel. Few men in the early republic equalled in wealth and status the likes of William Gray, Elias H. Derby, the Salem Crowninshields, Thomas H. Perkins of Boston, Nathan and Samuel Appleton from New Ipswich, and Amos and Abbott Lawrence from Groton—none of them college-educated. The distance from the bookish experience was even greater among entrepreneurs outside New England—John Jacob Astor, Cornelius Vanderbilt, Stephen Girard, Jay Cook, John D. Rockefeller, and Andrew

Carnegie. Strive to succeed, the standing advice to young men eager to gain wealth, meant immersal in work not in libraries.

Collegiate education was no more essential to success in politics than in business. In the seventeenth and eighteenth centuries involvement in government was a gentlemanly pursuit and Harvard counted among its alumni such public servants as Thomas Hutchinson (class of 1727) and Peter Oliver (class of 1730), as well as John Hancock and John (class of 1755) and Samuel Adams (class of 1740). But the more likely models for future leaders, Patrick Henry, George Washington, and John Marshall had needed no bachelor's degree to enter politics. In the nineteenth century, the link between education and achievement in public office weakened further—political heroes like Jackson, Lincoln, and Cleveland were then men of the people, not college-bred.

Did a concerned father wish to prepare his son for a career in law, medicine, teaching, engineering, or journalism? The college classroom was not the place for it. The means of advancing was rather experience gained through apprenticeship, which often had the additional advantage of making useful connections for the fledgling practitioner. Just before and just after 1800, formal schools of law, divinity, and medicine appeared in Cambridge and elsewhere; but their lectures generally supplemented rather than substituted for apprenticeship; and in any case none required their students first to have completed a college course.

Most parents dispatched their sons to Harvard as they long had to English universities not for vocational but for custodial reasons. They calculated, as Winthrop and de Merton had, that a pious atmosphere in which aspiring ministers lived under close supervision would tame or contain the restless spirits of lads in the awkward transition to adulthood. In both Oxford and Cambridge, the commoners or boarders had steadily grown more numerous. By the sixteenth century great men's families like the Verneys were sending their idle and dissolute sons to college to receive the *polite learning* appropriate to gentlemen, or at least to be trained in the rudiments of orderly life.

Puritan families felt the urgency with special intensity. Idleness, they knew, was the source of many evils; yet a well-to-do home offered few activities to a boy in his early teens, a period of high susceptibility to temptation. All too many parents, aware that their children made themselves vile, restrained them not and tolerated resistance to authority out of weakness or misguided affection. Cotton Mather (class of 1678), interviewing condemned criminals on the way to the gallows, traced their downfall commonly to disobedience to parents and ungovernableness. His father, Increase Mather (class of 1656), did what he could to forestall that fate for the "40 or 50 children" in the college when he became president. A century and a half later President Edward Everett (class of 1811) was disappointed to find himself "the sub-master of an ill-disciplined school" rather than head of the "most famous institution of learning in America." "While meditating high-sounding phrases about liberal education," he was obliged to reprove a senior for casting reflections with a looking glass on the face of a lady passing through the Yard. The hateful duty of questioning three students about their beckoning to loose women elicited a cry of agony: "Is this all I am fit for? . . . The life I am now leading must end, or it will end me."

"By doing nothing, men learn to do evil," a Puritan minister warned, whereas useful labor constrained natures "inclined to all manner of sins." For those who did not work with their hands, Harvard offered an alternative: subjection to a rigid and exhausting schedule that preempted the entire day and kept the boys out of trouble. The business of the institution was thus discipline. The very first Commencement (1642) saw two young gentlemen flogged for foul misbehavior, this after the departure of Nathaniel Eaton, "fitter to have been an officer in the inquisition, or master of a house of correction, than an instructor of Christian youth," who, besides, served his charges hasty pudding with goat's dung in it. The rod and the ferule after 1718 ceased to enforce obedience, in sharp contrast to English schools which, well into the nineteenth century, subjected boys of the same age to brutal beatings. Instead, Frederic H. Hedge complained in 1866, Harvard made lads recite lessons from textbooks and write compulsory exercises. Aside from an occasional box on the ears, fines and lesser punishments reinforced pleas for self-control. If, along the way, some lessons about the worth of moral discipline also sank in, that was all to the good.

The custodial function of the College met the needs of families unable to control sons between the ages of fourteen and eighteen. It made men of the boys. In 1798 when George Washington's step-grandson was having trouble in Princeton, the President decided to send the lad to Harvard in the belief that "the habits of the youth there, whether from the discipline of the school, or from the greater attention of the people generally to morals," were "less prone to dissipation and debauchery" than at the colleges south of it. When the Harvard President each year presented candidates for the bachelor's degree, he certified that they were polished in learning and in manners, the latter as important as the former. With some bitterness, Benjamin Franklin, not a college graduate, wrote in 1722 that parents send their boys to Harvard, "where for want of a suitable Genius, they learn little more than how to carry themselves handsomely, and enter a Room genteely (which might as well be acquired at a Dancing-school), and from whence they return, after abundance of trouble and Charges, as great Blockheads as ever, only more proud and self-conceited."

Franklin's indictment was unfair, but had an element of truth in it. For the objective of discipline shaped the quality of student life and the pattern of instruction in his day and until the second half of the nineteenth century. The president and tutors enforced the parietal rules and held their charges to a rigid schedule that ran from compulsory chapel in early morning on through the whole day. Recitations were less opportunities for instruction than means of checking the diligence of students in performing their exercises outside the classroom. John Davis Long (class of 1857) years later recalled four years of monotonous routine with no word of stimulus or encouragement. And the infamous scale of merit which infuriated Henry Adams (class of 1850) rested on marks for conduct combined with those for academic performance. His father, Charles Francis Adams (class of 1825) summed up the sentiments of a generation, not long after taking the degree: "Nothing came back to me that I valued." He recalled not a single warming association. "No Graduate of modern times whom I have met entertains any enthusiasm for the place of his education."

The young men, of course, had their own motives for attending, and those were not identical with the reasons of the college or of the

Student room.

Students at a meal, 1896.

Students, 1902.

Students, drinking, 1896.

parents. Love of learning always drew some, as it did Henry Dunster, a yeoman's son, or Ralph Waldo Emerson (class of 1821) and George Bancroft (class of 1817), the sons of poor ministers. For them study was attractive in its own right and also opened an escape from the poverty of home. Henry David Thoreau (class of 1837) turned up because he knew no other way of becoming the poet he intended to be.

But college offered most lads an escape of another sort—from family supervision and from precisely that discipline the parents sought to reinforce. To arrive in a strange town, to establish distance from familiar places and people, and to enter a community of peers in age and status was to discover independence, a process that called for the test of external authority. Part of the social history of the University in the eighteenth and nineteenth centuries could be written as a chronicle of riots and rebellion. But more often the chafing against external rules led to boyish disorder, sharpened by the pains of adolescence. Jones Very (class of 1836) as a student suffered from an unbridled but unsatisfied passion for women which he repressed by monkish austerity and self denial. Other youths played the devil in pranks or lost themselves in alcohol. Broken windows were the least of it. Charles Francis Adams, Jr. (class of 1856), an Overseer in the 1880s, need not have been surprised when he deplored the drunkenness he discovered at Commencement. At the Commencement of 1791 more than a hundred undergraduates fell simultaneously sick of an emetic someone had thrown into the breakfast water. Diverting would have been the scene, wrote an observer, were it not too serious to see the students—their minds recently crammed with elevated thoughts—now hanging their heads and puking about the Yard.

Until Eliot's era, the presidents were always the scapegoats for the failure of the system. After Holyoke's long term, it was difficult to find a hardy pedagogue willing to take on the responsibility. It was chapel, day in, day out. President Josiah Quincy (class of 1790) in 1845 had to explain to the Overseers that the three times he had missed morning prayers in sixteen years, he had been away on college business. They also wanted to know why he could not teach full time, do with one instructor less, and thus save $2,000 a year. The president had to prevent disorder with limited power and without community support. In the end, sooner or later, more or less, students had to be forgiven, "in consequence of their youth and probability that they proceeded without much reflection of the nature of the offense" (1808). Boys would be boys. In the last analysis, these were the sons of the University's patrons. It would not do permanently to alienate those whose generosity and tuition supported the institution. To placate the parents and students, it was often necessary to ease out the unyielding president and pretend some genuine issue of high principle was involved.

The case of President John Thornton Kirkland (class of 1789) demonstrated the difficulty of keeping a balance. Appointed in 1810 he soon earned a reputation as the best loved of presidents. There was no mystery why. A student song, the next decade, ran, "To jolly old Kirkland let us drink the first glass." Indulgence was his way to a boy's heart. Similar tactics won over the faculty. One teacher, writing to a friend, noted the great improvement under Kirkland's administration. "Instead of rancor and contention, we have the feast of reason and the flow of soul. When the business is dry and perplexing we are comforted with wine and cigars. In short, the whole face of things here is changed, and every way for the better." In time, however, the cigars ran out, and Kirkland's leniency led in due course to the great rebellion of 1823 and to his retirement. Josiah Quincy followed him and passed through a similar cycle. Presidential terms thereafter were short, about four years each, until Eliot's day.

The custodial function of the College explained its ambiguous attitude toward student life. As in all institutions, the keepers were always suspicious of the inmates. What were they up to? The question haunted the tutors. Boyish independence was laudable—but within limits. In 1800 the Corporation ruled that no class could hold a meeting without the president's permission. In 1809 it forbade any "illegal combinations."

As might be expected, the students responded by forming precisely such little organizations of their own, beginning with "speaking societies" in the eighteenth century. Greek letters and other arcane names created an impression of secrecy, indeed of mysteries known only to the initiates. The thrill of election added to the clubs' attractiveness—if some were chosen, others were excluded, which created hierarchical gradations that many boys regarded as more important than rank in class or academic honors. Hasty Pudding, Porcellian, Phi Beta Kappa, Pierian Sodality among others furnished students alternative autonomous activities that organized their lives.

What were they up to? The members met in one another's rooms, or they had quarters of their own. They ate and they drank, escaping the despised commons. They collected libraries; they read and discussed books and newspapers. They conducted literary and musical exercises; they wrote and published the products. They indulged in athletics. In short, they educated themselves in their own way, without supervision, and despite the penal curriculum to which the College subjected them. And the president and tutors, who certainly knew about these activities, discreetly tolerated them.

There was no such escape for instructors, chained as they were to parietal duties. Life for them was no more tolerable than for their charges. Low pay, disagreeable chores, routine, petty intrigue created a stifling environment; if they kept an eye on the boys, the much more numerous boys kept an eye on them. Of course, there had been the famous Henry Flynt (class of 1693), who served forty-nine years as tutor, less a model to be imitated than a premonitory lesson of the fate that awaited a young B.A. who could not find either a respectable parish or a rich wife. The ablest instructors taught for a few years while seeking one position or another and left with few regrets.

Generation after generation, a few teachers yearned for at least a corner of the Yard in which to nurse the plant of learning. For almost two hundred years only John Winthrop (class of 1732) succeeded. Sustained by impeccable status and by abundant means, he used the professorship of mathematics to introduce laboratory instruction and calculus and earned election to the Royal Society and an honorary doctorate from Edinburgh. His was a lonely eminence. His predecessor, Professor Isaac Greenwood (class of 1721), had been dismissed for "various acts of gross intemperance by excessive drinking." Leonard Hoar (class of 1650), president from 1672 to 1675 and holder of an M.D. degree, longed to build a chemistry laboratory and a botanical collection. But the students made his situation intolerable and compelled him to resign.

The great change of the eighteenth century, the era of enlightenment, was the provision passed in 1767 that arrayed teaching by subject instead of by class, thus permitting each tutor some degree of specialization. The reform suggested some regard for the content of instruction but not a shift away from the recitation as a disciplinary instrument. Joseph Willard (class of 1765) and Samuel Webber (class of 1784), who presided over this period, served out their terms without incident but also without achievement. Both were interested in mathematics and astronomy, but Webber's hope to erect an observatory yielded only a sun-dial as its monument.

Willard often expressed the wish, never to be granted, some day to visit the great European universities. A generation later, young scholars who had actually studied in Germany returned to teach at Harvard, hot for reform. But neither George Ticknor as professor nor Josiah Quincy as president could fundamentally alter the old ways, despite the wealth of the former and family connections of the latter. Another president who had studied in Germany in his youth sought other means of improvement during his brief tenure of office. Edward Everett presided at the creation of the Lawrence Scientific School, intended as a distinct, serious, and scholarly branch of Harvard. But it all too quickly degenerated into a means of dispensing non-classical and inferior degrees. In the opinion of some, including Charles William Eliot, the College struck bottom in 1853.

His two immediate predecessors, James Walker (class of 1814) and Thomas Hill (class of 1843), meant well and sincerely wished to make Harvard a "university in the highest and best sense." The odds were against them, as against other reformers, so long as Harvard remained a disciplinary institution devoted to making men of boys. The most significant venture away from the old pattern was the establishment of the University Lectures, detached from any curriculum and open to the public rather than primarily to students.

Harvard's failure also befell other, even more daring experiments at Union, Nashville, Brown and Michigan. Innovative administrators and teachers, their imaginations sparked by images from abroad, earnestly tried to refurbish the University as a scholarly institution, and all ran into the same insuperable obstacle: the American college was simply not congenial to scholarship. Harvard after 1850 numbered among its faculty some learned men who would have liked to do more than hear the boys recite. That, however, was not the purpose of the place.

The tradition of the autodidact in the United States inhibited the thought of an institutional setting for true learning. Knowledge was, no doubt, a good thing. Let him or her who cherished it seek it out— no better model than that of a Fellow of the Royal Society, Benjamin Franklin, whose Oxford doctorate recognized labors past rather than future promise. His townsman, the ingenious David Rittenhouse, the ornithologist J. J. Audubon and, closer to home, the navigator Nathaniel Bowditch demonstrated that learning—useful and ornamental—was within reach of those who had idled no time away in college.

Americans found two models particularly instructive. Benjamin Thompson, Count Rumford to be, was a farm boy from Woburn. Apprenticed at thirteen to a shopkeeper as was the custom, after five years he elevated his sights and decided to try medicine. A year later, at the age of nineteen, he once more widened horizons and married a rich widow. He enjoyed considerable success as bureaucrat, first in England and then on the continent of Europe, while all along devoting himself to science. Thompson experimented with gunpowder, propounded a new theory of heat, earned a title, and endowed a chemistry professorship at Harvard.

Thomas Dowse of Cambridge, by contrast, never became wealthy and never moved—upward or away. In 1856 he nevertheless bequeathed to the Massachusetts Historical Society a private library consisting of 5,000 volumes—fine editions in fine bindings. Dowse lived in Cambridge but was neither a professor nor a graduate of Harvard College. His education he got from his father whose calling he followed, and he earned his livelihood as a currier and a leather dresser.

Learning was what individuals did for the love of it, and it had little to do with the custody of boys. When Presidents Willard and Webber sought a broader context for their scholarship, they turned to the American Academy of Arts and Sciences of which they were members; this independent institution modelled on the European enlightenment societies seemed more appropriate than the College. The scientists who established the Museum of Comparative Zoology in 1858 did so through a separate corporation, as did the founders of the Institute of Technology three years later. In other parts of the country efforts to provide a setting for advanced teaching and research also took for granted the necessity of separating it from college work. The founders of Clark and The Johns Hopkins universities provided for no undergraduate college at all; and Chicago, Stanford, and Columbia entrusted the two kinds of teaching to separate faculties. President Woodrow Wilson of Princeton thought it plausible to situate the graduate school at a considerable distance from the undergraduate. But Charles W. Eliot believed both in serious graduate instruction and in undergraduate teaching provided by the same faculty in a university-college. To make that possible he had to transform the fashion in which Harvard turned boys into men.

In 1869, when Eliot became president, the teaching staff already included such distinguished scholars as the naturalists Louis Agassiz and Jeffries Wyman, the literati James Russell Lowell (class of 1838), Henry Wadsworth Longfellow, and Charles Eliot Norton (class of 1846), the mathematician Benjamin Peirce (class of 1829), the folklorist Francis J. Child, the classicist James B. Greenough, and the botanist Asa Gray. But although some of these luminaries were free to lecture in their respective fields, as teachers they also listened to recitations, assigned grades, and performed parietal duties—deadening routines inimical to creative work. Eliot's innovation, the elective system, liberated them to specialize and to lecture on the results of their scholarship. The division of undergraduates into classes disappeared except in social and extracurricular affairs. Instruction instead was organized in courses, assigned weight as units that students were free to assemble according to their own tastes and interests.

Perhaps Eliot really believed that in Harvard's pluralistic universe students would sort themselves out, voluntarily by taste and interest, so as to distribute themselves more or less equally among the offerings of their distinguished professors. Harsh contemporary critics, among them Presidents James McCosh of Princeton and Noah Porter of Yale, warned that the visionary scheme would not work, expecting failure yet fearing the infectious spread of the elective idea to their own institutions.

Of course the critics were correct. The reforms did not work in the sense that the students did not distribute themselves through the whole range of course offerings. In the academic year 1900–1901, for instance, 2,000 students registered in the Faculty of Arts and Sciences, taking four courses each—a total of 8,000 course enrollments. That year, the six largest classes enrolled 2,800 pupils or, in other words, did 35 percent of all the instruction. The eleven largest courses (each with 200 students or more) did one-half of all the teaching. A small group, a dozen or so of professors, well known for their performing skills, thus handled most of the College's instructional needs. Four hundred other courses enrolled an average of ten students; and the median was even smaller because some registered only one or two. In 1902–1903, the distinguished historian Charles H. Haskins attracted six, four, and one students in his three courses; his colleague, Edwin F. Gay, drew sixteen, eighteen, and four. Neither suffered any loss of esteem in the president's eyes.

Eliot's sleight of hand appeared to liberate the students; it gave them a choice few actually exercised, to range far and wide in an expanding curriculum. In actuality, reform freed the faculty for scholarship. Relieved of the chore of hearing recitations, those who wished could devote themselves to learning, with the instruction they offered a spin-off from their own thinking.

Moreover, the new system gave the students too a stake in scholarship. The faculty still worried about discipline; the *Annual Report* for 1903–1904 dilated on false excuses for cutting class and absences for pleasure trips and parties. But the process of making men of the boys now depended not on compulsory chapel, which ended in 1886, not on the rod or on rigid rules, not on prescribed schedules or on lessons in moral discipline, but on the free involvement in the culture of learning. The change transformed student life. Thomas W. Lamont (class of 1892), recalling in 1946 what made his four Harvard years happy, mentioned first, awareness "of the vast stores of learning and thought" made available to him; and then "the sense of freedom" in the atmosphere.

The ability to effect the reform depended in part upon the force of Eliot's personal qualities. But a change in the character of the student body eased his task. Chronologically, indeed, it ceased to consist of boys. After mid-century parents in the United States, unless pressed by poverty, no longer expected sons under twenty to earn livelihoods or choose careers. Exceptionally precocious younsters like Henry Safford, the "lightning calculator" (class of 1854), Boris Sidis (class of 1894), or Norbert Wiener (class of 1912), still gained admission early. But more generally, the age of entering freshmen advanced from fourteen to eighteen or more; the undergraduate student body became perceptibly older. New academies—St. Paul's (1856), Groton (1885), Middlesex (1901), and others—prepared the offspring of select families specifically for Harvard, performing the custodial functions that had earlier fallen to the College. Young men left such schools ready to handle the class work, advised on where to reside, on which courses to take, which activities to pursue and which clubs and cliques to join, and furnished with friends whose lives they would share in Cambridge and later.

The expanding College also welcomed a wider range of students after 1880. Improved high-school instruction throughout the country equipped all sorts of youths for an eastern, Harvard, education. The high repute of Eliot's institution now offset its earlier reputation as a center of radical Unitarianism or of manly high jinks and persuaded some parents of its superior value as against state and local alternatives. In 1870 the College enrolled seven Catholics and three Jews. (Women were not admitted.) Thereafter the number of Jews and Catholics increased notably, of blacks less so. But color did not prevent "all-American" William H. Lewis (class of 1895 law) from captaining the football team or Clement Morgan (class of 1890) from election as class orator; and W. E. B. Du Bois (class of 1890), in reflecting later on his happiness at Harvard, recalled invitations to the home of William James. The desire for personal improvement, a thirst for knowledge, the ambition to rise in the world by association with Harvard's prestige, the great names among the faculty, and the cultural reputation of Cambridge lured the young men there; and liberal reforms allowed each to pursue his own goals.

Eliot's inclination was to let students go their own ways not only in studies but also in extracurricular activities. He thus legitimized the informal as well as the formal features of college life. He knew that the sons of wealthy families did not mingle with the midwestern youngsters, much less with the commuters from the unfashionable Boston or Chelsea districts. In the new Gold Coast apartments, the fellows from the select private schools, clubmen linked to Boston society, cultivated the aloofness and good taste by which they distinguished themselves. Crew was their sport of preference; and occasionally they spent time on the *Crimson*, as did Franklin D. Roosevelt (class of 1904). There he found the most useful preparation for later public service and also the consolation for failure of election to the Porcellian. Passing grades, earned with the aid of thriving private tutoring schools, satisfied the gentlemen. Let them be. Only let them be an elite of taste, not mere snobs. They would someday inherit wealth and rise to positions of power. They ought to prepare for the wise exercise of their responsibilities. Little seeds planted amidst Harvard's pleasant surroundings would someday help them use power and wealth wisely as custodians of culture.

The miscellaneous others mattered also. Having come not to join clubs but out of devotion to the principle of choice, they were potential missionaries to the world, the means by which Harvard acted as a nursery of independent thinkers. Among them were men of talent, waiting for opportunity. New people had always in the past risen in the United States to positions of influence; they would continue to do so. Let them form their own Menorah society and try to mesh inherited with Harvard traditions. Let them debate in socialist clubs and explore new ideas; or let them do good through Phillips Brooks House. Everyone would benefit from an aristocracy of merit. Meanwhile it was the University's mission to make sure that the quest for opportunity was embedded in values that would ultimately serve society.

The potential for achievement spurred the young men on. In Eliot's final years, two members of the class of 1910 saw that the ability to use words acquired at Harvard might be an instrument of power—to do good, of course. Both were outsiders, one from the West, the other from New York. Neither had a chance of election to a final club, although John Reed would have liked it. Walter Lippmann, too bright to aspire, launched a frontal attack on these bastions of aristocracy. Reed, romantic, impulsive, dashed into journalism to shake the world, without much understanding of the issues about which he wrote. Lippmann, more introspective, more knowledgeable, also sought to exercise influence through journalism, but did so more successfully from behind the seats of power. These two shared little beyond a confidence in their own rightness and in the superiority of their judgments; and those qualities derived from the certainty of knowing the best that was implanted at Harvard while the College made men of the boys.

Of the boys! Not of the girls!

The gender issue did not arise while the College was primarily a custodial institution. Girls becoming women differed from boys becoming men and there was not so much merit in a Harvard education that any should come beating at its doors. The solitary female who inquired in 1849 found it inexpedient to apply for admission although she probably had a legal right to do so. Scholarship transformed the issue. The shift of emphasis to learning opened the question: why should not women who wished to do so learn also? Besides, access gained value as the bachelor's degree became increasingly a requirement for professional careers. Lame efforts to find a physiological basis for exclusion persuaded few. Respectable female scholars were familiar figures of the past; and anyone who challenged the intelligence of the sex had to confront a redoubtable array of Cambridge wives with their own means of refutation. Besides, Cornell, Johns Hopkins, and many respectable state universities suffered no ill effects from coeducation.

The stumbling block was not the capacity to learn but the social role of the College. At one point, a majority of candidates for the Board of Overseers expressed a willingness to admit women to the Medical School but not as undergraduates. The "annex" (1879), later Radcliffe College (1894), accommodated the desire to give girls an academic education equivalent to Harvard's, without disturbing the way of life that still aimed to make men of the boys by involvement in a male network of the culture of learning. That accommodation endured for almost a half century with little protest and to the manifest satisfaction of the participants.

DONALD FLEMING

Eliot's New Broom

Charles William Eliot (1834–1926), A.B. 1853, the greatest man in the history of Harvard, though by no means the greatest Harvard man, delivered his inaugural address as President of the University on October 19, 1869. It was not a great speech, for it did not add up to any one thing, but it was intermittently great in the best Emersonian style of blindingly luminous individual sentences.

🐿 . . . the young man of nineteen or twenty ought to know what he likes best and is most fit for. The community does not owe superior education to all children, but only to the *élite* . . . . The process of preparing to enter college under the difficulties which poverty entails is just such a test of worthiness as is needed.

🐿 The poverty of scholars is of inestimable worth in this money-getting nation.

🐿 The world knows next to nothing about the natural mental capacities of the female sex.

🐿 Two kinds of men make good teachers—young men and men who never grow old.

🐿 There are always old radicals and young conservatives.

🐿 It is very hard to find competent professors for the university.

63

Very few Americans of eminent abilities are attracted to this profession.

 A university cannot be managed like a railroad or a cotton mill.

 ... the Overseers should always hold towards the Corporation an attitude of suspicious vigilance. They ought always to be pushing and prying.

 The inertia of a massive University is formidable. A good past is positively dangerous, if it makes us content with the present and so unprepared for the future.

 On its invested funds the Corporation should be always seeking how safely to make a quarter of a percent more.

 The University must accommodate itself promptly to significant changes in the character of the people for whom it exists.

 To see every day the evil fruit of a bad appointment must be the cruelest of official torments.

 [The President] cannot force his opinions upon any body. A University is the last place in the world for a dictator. Learning is always republican.

 The future of the University will not be unworthy of its past.

Who was Charles William Eliot? To take first (Bostonian) things first, he was the grandson of the donor of the Eliot professorship of Greek, the son of the former Treasurer of Harvard, the first cousin of one of the Overseers that elected him, and the nephew of Professors Andrews Norton and George Ticknor on their wives' side, and consequently the first cousin of Charles Eliot Norton, and through his own first wife he was the brother-in-law of Francis Greenwood Peabody, whose mother—but one must stop somewhere. He was the right sort. To crown his fitness for presiding over Harvard's affairs, he was even the man that made it crimson—by buying red silk handkerchiefs to tie around the heads of himself and the other members of the Harvard crew in a boat race in June 1858. (They won.)

Professionally, Eliot passed for a chemist, who served as tutor and assistant professor at Harvard from 1854 to 1863. The students did not like him, then or later, and his scientific colleagues, particularly the godlike Louis Agassiz, despised him for setting up in a field of which he knew next to nothing. He was quite properly passed over

Charles W. Eliot, 1872.

Finding something to read in the College Library.

Dining in Memorial Hall.

for the Rumford professorship in 1863 and left Harvard. After a long roving tour of European universities, with an eye to noting educational practices rather than brushing up his chemistry, he became professor of chemistry at the new Massachusetts Institute of Technology in Boston. In 1868 he was elected a Harvard Overseer a few months before President Thomas Hill resigned. The presidency was refused by the first choice, Charles Francis Adams, the American minister to Britain during the Civil War; and Eliot was far from being everybody's second choice. In fact, the Overseers sent Eliot's nomination back to the Corporation. The deadlock was only broken by threatening Louis Agassiz, the main source of discontent, with a clergyman if he would not swallow Eliot. Agassiz preferred a bad scientist to a good clergyman and the deed was done.

Eliot himself said that he shared the apprehensions of those who had opposed him, and he worried about something that did not trouble them—a very large and highly visible birthmark on one of his cheeks, of the kind technically known as a port-wine stain. While his election was pending, he asked his best friend whether a man so marked could occupy the presidency without disgracing Harvard. All his posed photographs are in profile and taken from the good side. He need not have worried about inspiring public respect. He was a handsome man except for the birthmark, straight as a ramrod till he died at ninety-two, and endowed with an unforgettable deep voice, Freudianly described by one of his contemporaries (who hated him) as having a port-wine richness. Another, younger, contemporary, a professor of Greek history, said that when he tried to imagine the ascendancy that Pericles had achieved over the Athenians in their vast democratic assemblies, the only thing that made it conceivable was to have known President Eliot, for he too could have dominated any random assembly on any theme.

How exactly did he function as president? In the beginning, like some of his successors, he had to disarm the people who hadn't wanted him by sharing power with one of his recent rivals for the presidency—a historian, whom he appointed as first dean of the faculty of Harvard College (in 1870). It was the first serious recognition that the president could no longer do everything himself; and in line with this Eliot announced in 1873 that he had already begun the practice of formally consulting the existing professors on appointments and promotions in their departments. There is no doubt, however, that through his entire forty years as president, Eliot himself made the final decision about all appointments and had no qualms about overriding the advice that he had solicited, particularly if the advice was affirmative and he was negative. But how did he find out that he was negative? Partly by encouraging interminable faculty meetings. George Santayana had some heartfelt reflections on these.

> The Faculty meetings were an object lesson to me in the futility of parliamentary institutions. Those who spoke spoke badly, with imperfect knowledge of the matter in hand, and simply to air their prejudices. The rest hardly listened. If there was a vote, it revealed not the results of the debate, but the previous and settled sentiments of the voters. The uselessness and the poor quality of the whole performance were so evident that it surprised me to see that so many intelligent men—for they were intelligent when doing their special work—should tamely waste so much time in keeping up the farce.

Yet Eliot found the meetings extremely useful in a way that even Santayana might have relished if he had known. In the midst of the genial pomposities attending the celebration of Eliot's ninetieth birthday, he mischievously revealed all:

> . . . in listening to debates in the Faculty and in inviting my opponents to speak, I was . . . pursuing with a good deal of perspicacity a study of those men . . . making up my mind whether these zealous opponents were of the right stuff to be made professors in Harvard University. That is just what I was doing.

By this and many other means, Eliot formed some very harsh opinions of faculty members, but these generally had a solid if insufficient foundation. He never had any respect for Charles Townsend Copeland (at Harvard from 1893), the rapidly-becoming-legendary "Copey," who taught a sophomore course in English composition but owed his greatest vogue, in and out of the College, to public readings of Dickens, Kipling, and the Bible—occasions unkindly described by a colleague as Copey's "spiritual debauch." Eliot rightly thought that Copey was no scholar and too much of a showman. Another man, of a very different cast, the philosopher Santayana,

66

aroused deep misgivings in Eliot on grounds of personality and character. At the time when Santayana's promotion to assistant professor was being discussed, Eliot wrote of him:

> The withdrawn, contemplative man who takes no part in the everyday work of the institution or of the world, seems to me a person of very uncertain value. He does not dig ditches, or lay bricks, or write school-books, his product is not of the ordinary, though humble kind. What will it be? It may be something of the highest utility; but, on the other hand, it may be something futile, or even harmful because unnatural and untimely.

This tells as much about Eliot as about Santayana, but Eliot has accurately caught the chilly detachment from Harvard that Santayana revealed as soon as he could afford it. The real point about Eliot's distaste for Copeland and Santayana was that he kept them both at Harvard notwithstanding his personal antipathies. He never let Copeland advance beyond instructor, but that was the predominant desire in the English Department itself; and Santayana, who was strongly backed by the philosophers, was rapidly promoted to full professor after Eliot was induced to swallow the first dose of him. It speaks volumes about the time and place, as well as about Eliot, that the key words that had to be invoked by the Philosophy Department on Santayana's behalf were "wholesome," "strong," and "healthy," and if they had meant that he was going to live a long time, they were right.

Was Eliot never vindictive? He did transfer the distinguished chemist who had beaten him out for the Rumford professorship to the Physics Department, thereby depriving him of an adequate laboratory and leaving him substantially high and dry though perfectly secure in his tenure.

In the matter of retaining and promoting non-tenured faculty members, Eliot was constrained not only by his sense of fairness but also by the implicatons of the great educational reform with which his name will always be associated—the doctrinaire application of the elective system to all undergraduate teaching. When Eliot had worked his will in this matter, he had to bow to the results of the Darwinian competition among instructors that he had set up. The men who could pack the students in, or at any rate had them begging for admission to courses with limited enrollments, could not easily be dismissed. Conversely, as seen from the side of teachers trying to get a start, the desperate quest for student popularity endemic in modern (i.e., Eliotized) American universities had begun. The students adored Copey from the beginning and not even Eliot could shake him off. But Santayana in his early days was a notoriously bad teacher, entitled to quake in his shoes when Eliot stopped him in the Yard to inquire about the students in his courses. Santayana started to say that they seemed keen and responsive, but Eliot interrupted him impatiently, as if Santayana was about to waste his time: "I meant, *what is the number of students* in your classes." Santayana soon became popular with students and impossible to dislodge, but the lesson was clear— keep up your enrollments or perish. When Henry Cabot Lodge was teaching American history down to 1840 and the enrollment plummeted from 50 to 3, he was well advised to read the writing on the wall and go into politics, where tedious discourses are seldom penalized. Eliot did think that all significant new fields of scholarship ought to be promptly incorporated in the Harvard curriculum as they emerged or differentiated themselves, and this entailed glorying in a good many increasingly specialized professors with inevitably minuscule constituencies; but all the more reason to keep track of rival instructors in traditional fields who could justly be held to the Darwinian test of surviving the undergraduates' scrutiny of Eliot's smorgasbord.

The tacit introduction of student suffrages into the promotions policy of the University was only one of the almost infinite reverberations of Eliot's unqualified embrace of the elective system. It therefore becomes essential to discover why he took it up in the first place and where else it led him. As Eliot never tired of repeating, he certainly did not invent the idea of electives at Harvard. One of the few things that George Ticknor—Eliot's uncle-by-marriage—salvaged from his grandiose plans of 1825 for reforming the curriculum was the introduction of electives in his own Modern Languages Department, where they were never displaced. But except for this, electives made very little headway at Harvard in the following generation.

It was Eliot's own generation as a student and he and many of his contemporaries hated it with a slow-burning rage unequalled till the end of the 1960s. The one experience that redeemed his undergraduate career, and conceivably his entire life, was to be taken by what he called "personal kindness" into the private laboratory of the professor of chemistry, Josiah Parsons Cooke, "Jopey" Cooke, and enabled to "learn what the process of scientific experimentation and search for truth was." The only thing that kindled his imagination as an undergraduate was the one task that he had undertaken voluntarily and plugged away at for three years with no recognition from the College. He was still grateful for this experience on his ninetieth birthday:

> My friends, I was the only undergraduate between 1849 and 1853 who had any such blessing. It was a sense of this privilege that first enlisted me, when I became a teacher of Harvard College, in the advocacy of choice among studies. . . .

In his own time as a Harvard teacher, from 1854 to 1863, little progress was made in this direction; but when he returned as president he found that the logjam had broken and President Hill had begun to move toward electives. There were excellent reasons why Eliot consistently tried to share the credit and blame for electives with his predecessor (whom he admired). In the first place, it was just; in the second place, it was strategic. But one must not be confused by Eliot's smokescreen. There was a quantum jump from increasing the number of electives to making a student's entire program elective, from letting up on requirements to abolishing them across the board. The latter was what Eliot accomplished by stages, working downward from the Senior year to the Freshman, till in 1885 the *only* remaining requirements were English composition and either French or German. As he rather complacently put the matter: "None of the former exclusive staples, Greek, Latin, mathematics, logic, and metaphysics, are required, and no particular combinations or selections of courses are recommended by the faculty." It was a revolution, and so intended.

Modern revolutionaries generally try to invoke historical necessity. Eliot always said that even in 1869 the faculty was simply too *big* to be utilized in a required curriculum. If there was to be only one curriculum for all students, he was right and that was certainly the basic tradition at Harvard; but alternative curricula, each with its own rigid requirements, could easily have been devised to press more faculty members into service. The fact is that Eliot was a doctrinaire of freedom for students and he was not looking for any compromises with the old system:

> . . . a well-instructed youth of eighteen can select for himself— not for any other boy, or for the fictitious universal boy, but for himself alone—a better course of study than any college faculty, or any wise man who does not know him and his ancestors and his previous life, can possibly select for him. In choosing his course he will naturally seek aid from teachers and friends who have intimate knowledge of him, and he will act under the dominion of that intense conservatism which fortunately actuates civilized man in the whole matter of education, and under various other safeguards which nature and not arbitrary regulation provides.

Among these other safeguards, Eliot included the internal logic of any field of study, leading a person on from one thing to the next, and what he called the "prevailing tendency on the part of every competent student to carry far any congenial subject once entered upon." He was totally unfazed when asked what would become of "the careless, indifferent, lazy boys who have no bent or intellectual ambition of any sort?" He replied that such boys never profited from any educational régime, and least of all, as he could testify from personal observation, from the old compulsory system at Harvard—in the words of one of his sympathizers, "in vain was the dunce Hellenized, in vain the drone Latinized." Besides, Eliot was ruthless about such students. "It really does not make much difference," he said, "what these unawakened minds dawdle with." He added that there was a better chance of their getting mildly interested in *something* under the elective system. Anyhow, they would be less truculent about the whole thing, and present fewer disciplinary problems. Eliot may have underestimated the numbers of these men under the new dispensation, but he knew that the phenomenon was eternal. He was a revolutionary but no utopian.

His real concern was always for an *élite* of intellect and character, recruited from all levels of society but smoothed and polished by the distinctively Harvard infusion of young aristocrats, representatives of the family stocks that had been recurring at Harvard for a century or more. "Equality of condition" was not a desirable or feasible goal for the American or any other republic—that was an unsound "French" ideal rather than a wholesome "Anglo-Saxon" aspiration—but the minority of families scrambling up into the *élite* and staying there could be slowly increased. Ideally, they could be imbued with feelings of "unity" toward the bulk of their fellow citizens while candidly rising above them in manners and tastes and endeavoring to transmit their legitimate superiority to their descendants. Unfavorable specimens of their own kind would inevitably be winnowed out in every generation.

Yet Eliot never thought that even the *élite* of brains and character could find their way to self-fulfillment and social utility without the aid of external stimuli—not requirements but seductive stimuli. In his view, the principal carrot for enticing the students forward was the system of honors already initiated by the faculty in 1866–67 under President Hill, supplemented in 1879 by a lesser distinction known as "honorable mention." A university, said Eliot, "must provide academic honors at graduation for distinguished attainments in single subjects."

Eliot inherited the honors system, but in his opinion there was something lacking to make it work, which he consciously undertook to foster—the creation of genuine academic departments as we understand the term. Nominal departments had long existed as a device for categorizing the individual members of the faculty, and the people in a given category had sometimes interacted, though not necessarily, but the departments had never pretended to be continuously functioning administrative units concerting educational programs. Mere listing of courses by departments, almost inseparable from the electives revolution, began as early as the catalogue of 1870–1871. But, as Eliot pointed out, the crux of the matter was the honors program:

> It is an incidental advantage of the [honors] system that the organization of departments of instruction is promoted by it. The teachers of Latin, of history, or of philosophy, find it necessary to arrange their courses in orderly sequence, to compare their methods and their results, and to enrich and diversify as much as possible the instruction which they collectively offer.

A sense of collective responsibility to students was the new ingredient. And for Eliot the logical web was seamless—the elective system required honors programs and honors programs required departments. He was obviously trying to encourage departments from the early 70s on, but their unbroken history and prescriptive rights date from the founding of the Faculty of Arts and Sciences in 1890, entailing the incorporation of the faculty of the Lawrence Scientific School in the faculty of Harvard College. Administrative historians may wish to know that no departmental minutes exist before 1891, which is probably the test. In later times, departments have frequently been seen as bastions of conservatism; but historically they were perceived by one of the best judges as an indispensable accompaniment to the elective system, an integral part of the greater freedom to follow their own bent that Eliot was striving to confer upon undergraduates—not a trammel upon their spirits but a means of clearing channels for them.

The elective system and the honors program combined—and Eliot always saw them as a combination—to create an inexorable demand for a new conception of university libraries, both as physical structures and as human environments. One essential step, opening entirely new vistas for accessibility to libraries, had been taken as early as 1861, the creation by Ezra Abbot of a public card catalogue at Harvard. But beyond this, if students were taking courses because they were interested in them—always making ample allowance for the vital role of gut courses in an elective system; the first great gut seems to have been Nathaniel Shaler's Geology ("all the geology necessary to a gentleman")—and still more if they were working for honors, they needed and wanted to get at more and more books in more and more areas. Henry Adams in his professorial phase (1870–1877) seems to have invented the idea of reserved books for courses. When his students complained that there weren't enough tables to sit at while reading the books, he found that many tables were being used by the library staff for miscellaneous storage and is reputed to have said: "Unless you clear your junk away in three days, I will take this up with my friends on the Corporation." The junk was cleared away and the students entered into their own. But reserved books were not enough. Interested students wanted to use all the books in the library, and they wanted the library to have all the books there

Mermaid Club, 1888.
(George Santayana seated at left).

Harvard Lampoon

Gore Hall reading room.

were. When Eliot came in, this was physically impossible. Harvard had probably the best library building of any university in the country—Gore Hall, erected in 1841, a pseudo-Gothic structure that figures in the seal of the City of Cambridge and also in a bas-relief set into the front wall of Widener Library, which replaced it in 1915. The trouble with Gore Hall, apart from the fact that it was certified to be full as early as 1863, was that it was designed on the then prevalent alcove principle, with each category of books shelved in its own alcove. As a scheme for storing books, it was enormously wasteful of space; as a scheme for supplying access to them, it funneled people in and out of little niches; as a scheme for accommodating new accessions, it could only slop over with the maximum inconvenience from one alcove into another. It was more than an inconvenience. Eliot's Harvard wouldn't work unless the library bottleneck was smashed once and for all.

The solution to this was one of the notable inventions of the nineteenth century, foreshadowed in the shelving arrangements for the Reading Room of the British Museum (completed in 1857) but first brought to perfection in recognizably modern form in an addition to Gore Hall in 1876—the bookstack, a narrow-aisled system of free-standing iron uprights, extending uninterruptedly from the foundations to the top floor, adapted to bearing adjustable shelves and supporting the entire weight of the floors, roof, shelving, and books. The external walls were aptly described as a mere "shell." It was the "skyscraper" principle of construction applied to library shelving—in advance of skyscrapers themselves, for the first of these wasn't put up till 1883–1884.

The architecturally and bibliothecally innovating structure tacked on to Gore Hall was conceived by two men, Justin Winsor, about to become the Harvard librarian, and the architect Henry Van Brunt, chiefly remembered and sometimes execrated as one of the designers of Memorial Hall. But some doubts were felt about the stability of a bookstack with six floors, and Eliot himself deserves credit for authorizing its construction. The gamble paid off in the most flexible, compact, and accessible form of shelving books that had ever been known. This and everything else that Justin Winsor was connected with at Harvard was pointed to the revolutionary principle that "books should be used to the largest extent possible and with the least trouble." That suggested one more step and he took it. He is the man who opened the stacks to students.

Liberal access to the stacks was merely one emblem of the trusting attitude toward students that pervaded Eliot's Harvard in a degree that was unprecedented in America. This attitude was obviously built into the elective system from the beginning; but even Eliot can hardly have foreseen its full implications for the disciplinary process. One form of preventive discipline under the old system had been the almost automatic knowledge, bolstered by rigorous attendance records and daily recitation grades, of where every student ought to be at every hour of instruction. Students could still behave outrageously in and out of the classroom, but they could not readily drift away from the educational grind. When wholesale electives came in, it was much easier for absentees to escape notice—one could always assume that they were under somebody else's charge. Moreover, the whole thrust of the Eliot days was toward greater freedom and voluntary attendance for juniors and seniors became common. On top of this, the elective system permitted an almost indefinite enlargement of the undergraduate body, in which Eliot revelled complacently, and the proportion of students who could be housed in the College, even if they wanted to, declined. Students who lived off campus—resplendently on the "Gold Coast," miserably in many little holes and crannies around Cambridge—were invisible to the college authorities for much of the day and all night. They had escaped from continuous discipline. They would probably be head over heels in trouble before the College found out.

The only sensible response, though rather belatedly acquiesced in, was to accept the fact that henceforth discipline at Harvard would be largely retrospective, meting out justice after the event, if then; and to favor a new type of personality for enforcing it. The man and the occasion were well met in Le Baron Russell Briggs, dean of Harvard College from 1891 to 1902, the greatest occupant of the office to date, and one of Eliot's most inspired appointments. Eliot said, typically, that he knew Briggs was the right man for the job because he had known his parents. Briggs's strategy, though that is putting the matter much too cynically, was to make himself liked and trusted by undergraduates, so that they would take their medicine gracefully if need be and clear out without creating a ruckus.

He'll kick you out of college, and he'll never shed a tear,
But he does it so politely that it's music to the ear.
He meets you in the anteroom, he grasps you by the hand,
He offers you the easy chair, and begs you not to stand.
"Good morning, Mr. Sporticus! How is your Uncle Jim?
I used to know him well at school—you look so much like
  him!
And you're enjoying college? Yes? Indeed! I am so glad!
Let's see—six *E*'s? Impossible! How very, very, sad!"
[By Henry Ware Eliot—from *Harvard Celebrities*]

Undergraduates in hot water knew that with rare exceptions Briggs would let them work their passage back by good conduct in the outside world. They also knew that he much preferred to keep them at Harvard if he could possibly justify it; and by an answering act of faith, many students sought him out before their problems had become irretrievable. He became the greatest single force at Harvard for inspiring the self-discipline of free men.

Even this was not the end of the freedoms initiated at Harvard under Eliot. In 1885 a group of undergraduates petitioned the governing boards to abolish compulsory attendance at chapel as "a remnant of ancient encroachments on civil liberty" and therefore tyrannical and unjust. A committee of Overseers replied that this was no more tyrannical than requiring attendance at classes (which, however, they must have known was becoming less common at Harvard) and besides Harvard could "ill afford the loss of reputation that would ensue in its being the first of all literary institutions in New England to abandon religious observances." The Overseers voted 20 to 4 to accept this report and they and the students seemed to be headed for a collision. But the new Plummer Professor of Christian Morals, Eliot's brother-in-law by his first marriage Francis Greenwood Peabody, electrified the community by declaring that he agreed with the students. Compulsory attendance at chapel was "repugnant" and "unjust." He made perfectly clear that he saw the connection between this issue and everything else that was happening in Eliot's Harvard. "The dogma of the University," said Peabody, "is now 'Discipline through Liberty.' "

The Corporation abolished compulsory chapel in 1886, with

elaborate arrangements to keep voluntary chapel going and to make it more attractive. The bland popular preacher Phillips Brooks drew from this the oddly Kierkegaardian but also Eliotian comfort that if even fifty young men turned up voluntarily to say their prayers every morning, it would be "the largest daily Protestant congregation in the world." The operative word was "Protestant." The elective system in secular and theological matters alike was the final consummation of Protestantism, and where should this inexorably unfold but in the most Protestant of universities. God had become an elective at Harvard. Where else? Why not?

Harvard's Golden Age?

Eliot's Harvard had jelled by about 1890 and with one arguable exception he did not conspicuously undertake to alter its fundamental character in the twenty remaining years of his tenure. Yet even in this period of consolidation, the Harvard environment was being inexorably transformed by the sheer increase in numbers. Eliot's principal blind spot was his incapacity or unwillingness to recognize that continually increasing numbers might affect the *quality* of life at Harvard, and not necessarily for the better.

Here are the actual statistics. The teachers of professorial grade in Harvard College grew from 45 in 1868–1869, the year before Eliot came in, to 90 in 1888–1889, and then to 194 in 1908–1909, when Eliot went out; and for comparative purposes to 469 in 1928–1929, when Lowell's presidency was waning in turn. As for undergraduates, there were 570 in 1868–1869, 1215 in 1888–1889, 2277 in 1908–1909, and 3486 in 1928–1929. Many people who lived through these times in Cambridge thought that the difference between having 150 classmates and having 580 was the difference between living in a humanly apprehensible situation that everybody could share and, alternatively, huddling together for warmth in mutually exclusive miniature Harvards that had less and less in common. But even if people who stayed on in Cambridge or Boston for twenty or thirty years were right in feeling that Harvard had become increasingly heterogeneous, the number of students crept up gradually. No one man would have noticed any particular change in numbers in his own time as an undergraduate.

Suppose you are a member of some class between 1900 and 1910. What are the main possibilities of student life in Cambridge? In the first place, who and what are you? You are probably older than Eliot thinks you ought to be—the average is 19 on entrance. There is a good chance, however, that you will make up for this by graduating in 3 years—no fewer than 36 percent of the class of 1906. Tom Eliot and Walter Lippmann are frequently going to be listed with the glorious class of 1910, with which they entered, but actually they will both complete the requirements for the A.B. a year in advance. The trick is to work off some (numerical) requirements by your entrance examinations and then to take an overload of courses each semester. But Eliot's aspiration to make the A.B. a three-year degree for everybody has been spiked by the increasingly looming figure of Professor A. Lawrence Lowell, who can prove from your choice of electives that most of your classmates are superficial smatterers doing very little work and needing no further encouragement to spread yourselves thin.

You really should have gone to a private school (sometimes known to those who have as a 'fitting school'), and you probably did—at any rate, 80 percent of your classmates did. The best thing is to enter from Groton or St. Paul's, though Andover or Exeter will do. If, however, you belong to the 20 percent that actually went to high school, you take such comfort as you can from occasional glimpses of America's golden youth at their childish pranks—the boys from St. Paul's throwing crusts at each other and butter at the ceiling.

You may be a German Jew but if you went to a good school (which is possible) and don't look or act particularly Jewish, that will cause no scandal though no rejoicing either. Santayana as an undergraduate in the 80s had been relieved to have a German-Jewish classmate *say* that he was Jewish, thereby obviating "pitfalls" in their relationship, though one wonders what these might have been and there is at least a hint that such candor was refreshing. Santayana describes this particularly cultivated acquaintance, eventually a generous benefactor of the Fogg Museum, as "rather friendless" at

A student at ease, 1889.

Harvard Banjo Club.

Purchasing tickets to the Harvard-Yale baseball game, 1901.

Harvard; but then his father was a dry-goods merchant into the bargain, and it may have been the combination that was lethal.

You may very well be a Russian or Polish Jew, and that is too much. Bernard Berenson of the class of 1887 was taken up by Boston society, but he was special (angelically beautiful for one thing), and now there are too many of you to be regarded as an appealing novelty. Owen Wister's nasty little novel about Harvard, *Philosophy 4* (1903), revolves about the contrast between the clean-cut and playful Bertie Rogers and Billy Schuyler, whose parents "owned town and country houses in New York," and the greasy grind Oscar Maironi, strongly implied to be Jewish though never labelled as such, whose parents "had come over in the steerage." Oscar, whose deepest instincts are for property and self-aggrandizement, lives in a "cheaper room" and eats "cheaper meals" than necessary, relieved by "sly times" in Boston when he "thoroughly ceased to be ascetic." He unavailingly tutors the feckless Bertie and Billy, but they, who are capable of learning from experience (having nothing else to go by), do better on the big philosophy examination than Oscar himself, the inveterate bookworm and note-taker.

All kinds of Jews together, and many of them are certainly more palatable than Oscar with his curled-up shoes and rusty suits, are going to soar from about 7 percent of the undergraduate enrollment in 1900 to 21 percent of 1922. If you are one of them, you will have to be obtuse not to grasp that many people are discreetly worried about whether the likes of you will ever level off. Professor Barrett Wendell is perfectly clear that the annual dinner in his own house for the Wendell Scholars in the College will have to be quietly abandoned if a Jew ever turns up among them.

Let alone a Negro; for you *may* be black, though that is highly improbable. If so, you are not forbidden to live in the Yard, but you are expected in the general course of things to see the wisdom of tucking yourself away somewhere else, though free and even encouraged to take your meals in Mem. Hall. That is why, if you are not black but white, you are probably not from the South. Where you probably are from is New England, New York, or Pennsylvania; and if not, you are far more likely to come from San Francisco than from Minneapolis.

Wherever you come from, you need a place to sleep. The College does not have nearly enough dormitory space and isn't making any serious effort to supply it. If you and one of your friends can get a room in Matthews, which is known as "chumming" rather than "rooming" together, you probably have an equally good friend who would like to be in the Yard too but has to live in a Cambridge rooming house, presided over by a respectable landlady. You cannot band together to rent a house of your own—that is an infraction of the college rules, though if you are desperately poor and get a chance to live in an unheated house free to keep it occupied, and Dean Briggs finds out, he won't say anything. If you're rich, there is an ideal solution, at least from a sybaritic point of view—the luxury apartment buildings put up after 1876 by private enterprise on the "Gold Coast," more or less in the vicinity of the later Adams House, some of which have actually been incorporated in it. In Walter Lippmann's formula, it's Mount Auburn Street or nowhere. But if you are Franklin D. Roosevelt—and you could be—you will live for a time in a handsome granite apartment building on Dunster Street.

Even if you can't swing that kind of comfort, you can still take your meals in the comparative luxury of Mem. Hall, where everybody who can has his own little dining group, which is how you keep up your friendship with the boy that got squeezed out of the Yard. There is a gallery looking down into the dining space, and everybody agrees that if you are stuck with a friend or relative who wants to see the sights of Cambridge—that eternal and probably intractable problem, given the limited amount of time that can be devoted to glass flowers—the only thing to do is to treat him to a view of the animals feeding in Mem. Hall. After you have taken a little European history, you will probably conclude that with the possible exception of Louis XIV, you and your chums are the most spied-upon trenchermen in history. It is not all a loss, for the galleries at Mem. Hall are open to anybody, and some Cambridge chippies may signal to you to meet them outside. They probably aren't that, just brash Irish girls with a snappy line of chatter who like to stroll through the Yard of an evening; and to be fair, you sometimes take the initiative by yelling at them from your window-seat. They are astonished to have attracted your notice.

If you are tired of eating in Mem. Hall and don't want to nip into Boston for a meal, your only recourse in Harvard Square is the Holly

Tree, a pallid little spot on tea room lines, where Copey may order you to vacate his regular seat. If you live in the Yard, you almost certainly have a fireplace in your room and probably make toast and tea and other little nibbles and gulps at your own fireside. The tea is a minor problem, for water has to be fetched from the cellar or the College Pump—the lordly thing is to make it worth the janitor's while to keep you supplied with water and coal for your fireplace, and throw in something extra for blacking your boots. The chances are that the fireplace is more than an amenity, for many of the dormitories in the Yard have no central heating in your time. And the reason you did not fetch the water for your tea from the john on your floor is that there is no plumbing above the basement. It is your much younger brother in the 1920s whom Copey asks to stand guard and see that nobody flushes the toilet on his floor while he is entertaining the (highly respectable) actress who rose superior to the name of Minnie Maddern Fiske.

In view of the rudimentary plumbing, one cannot be sure that you have had a bath today. Everybody seems to agree that in the 1880s you would hardly ever have bathed at all. But now luxury, not to say decadence, is creeping in, the apartments on the Gold Coast always have a bathroom on every floor, and one building has a private bath for each tenant. Most of your classmates don't aspire to be as effete as that, but the trouble is that you are getting more and more sweaty at athletics. If you go to the Hemenway Gymnasium, you will certainly have a shower before dressing for the street; and you are beginning to think that there ought to be a shower, and incidentally a toilet, on every floor in the Yard. Meanwhile, you can go to the cellar, where showers are beginning to be hooked up, or sponge off in your room. An occasional faculty member living in the Yard actually has a little bathtub, normally concealed under his bed and filled by ladling cold water into it with a dash of hot from the kettle; but the Irish "goodies" who do the daily cleaning make laughable fools of themselves by not knowing what it is, and one of them uses it to empty the slops from the night jars. You do have electric light.

After you have or have not dusted yourself off in the morning, there is an increasing chance that you will give yourself a clean shave, for men of your age are beginning to rebel against beards, and to a lesser extent mustaches, as the mark of stuffy old mossbacks trying to keep a lid on things. You still have to get dressed and you *always* wear a jacket and necktie—you would not be permitted in classrooms otherwise, but it probably never occurs to you to do anything else and you even loll about in your room with no further concession to informality than loosening your tie. You also wear a hat much of the time and frequently clench a pipe between your teeth to increase your masculinity quotient. The unlamented William Randolph Hearst had smoked long cigars in the Yard, but that was bad form and indicative of the cad that he was. The College doesn't purport to be prohibitionist, and you probably do drink—beer almost certainly, whiskey and champagne in the clubs and occasionally even in the dormitories. Van Wyck Brooks ('08) likes to tell how he went to a "punch" in Holworthy on the evening of his first day as a freshman, at the cry of "Bottoms up" drained a tumbler of straight whiskey that somebody had handed him, and promptly keeled over. Drinking is one of the electives too, and successful completion of the course consists in learning how much you can handle while approximately remaining a gentleman and avoiding the attention of the cops. To complete the picture of a collegiate man-of-the-world, you probably have or aspire to a bull-terrier—dogs are rife in the Yard, for there are no rules against them.

You can hardly be aware that after all your sartorial efforts, Professor Santayana thinks that you and most of your classmates look like shop-assistants, but you probably wouldn't care about this anyhow unless you care so much that you have your doubts about him. In any event, you have probably heard that Charles Eliot Norton used to trump everybody's ace in this regard by telling his genteel idolaters, "I daresay none of you have ever seen a gentleman."

Santayana may still have been living in the Yard himself when you were a freshman or sophomore, and this is one of the distinctive things about Harvard in your time. There are eminent senior men on the faculty making bachelor headquarters in the Yard. You are, alas, too young to have known Professor Evangelinus Apostolides Sophocles, a native of Thessaly who migrated to Harvard, where he taught Greek and generated legends from 1842 and lived on into the 1880s in Holworthy. You certainly know the famous stories about "Old Sophy"—how a proctor rushed up officiously to report that a student had cheated on his bluebook and Sophy said, "It make no matter. I nevare look at his book anyhow,"—how he gave the same grade to two boys, one of whom had swotted like the devil and the other had done nothing, and on being asked for an explanation replied, "You all do know nothing equally,"—and above all how he kept a pet chicken in his room in Holworthy and on his deathbed declined to drink some chicken-broth on the grounds that "You do not devour the one you love." (It wasn't the same chicken.)

Old Sophy is gone, and Santayana, who lived in Thayer, Stoughton, and Hollis successively, is going or gone in your time; but Copey—Charles Townsend Copeland—will still be there in 1932. He began in Grays 24 and in your time is living in Stoughton 7 (where Santayana had lived before him) or Hollis 15. Hollis 15 is a room with a considerable history—the previous occupants include Ralph Waldo Emerson, Charles William Eliot, and Charles Francis Adams, the Civil War minister to Britain. (Santayana lived in Hollis 19). You are undoubtedly going to bore people for the rest of your life with wonderful stories about Copey, but their charm seems to be evanescent. Perhaps your greatest success in this line is the one about his disgust at the blundering efforts of a baby learning to walk: "This is the most revolting exhibition of ineptitude that I have ever watched."

The important thing about Copey and the other members of the dwindling band of professors-in-the-Yard is the opportunity they give you to meet distinguished older men whom you admire, on highly informal terms. There are some magical places right in the Yard where your dreams of hearing interesting people talk about interesting things can actually come true. Copey's "Wednesday evenings after ten," when he holds open house, are the Harvard undergraduates' salon. He may invite you to meet Minnie Maddern Fiske, though probably not, but he will certainly see that you get to meet glamourous upperclassmen like Jack Reed from Oregon or Walter Lippmann. When these favorites are present, there is a good deal of chaffing between them and Copey, which is an eye-opener to you, and he does not seem to mind that Jack Reed has written a rather double-edged poetic tribute to him in the *Lampoon*:

> Don't your acolytes distress you,
> In their circle Johnsonese?
> Vying which shall cry "God bless you!"
> When you sneeze?

Some of your more severely intellectual classmates look down on Copey's Wednesdays as miscellaneous and undiscriminating. They hope to be invited home by Professor George Herbert Palmer of the Philosophy Department, whose wife Alice Freeman Palmer is as famous as he is and a former president of Wellesley. But the ultimate accolade is to be invited, as Van Wyck Brooks and his sidekick Max Perkins are, to one of the legendary Dante readings that Charles Eliot Norton, though retired, still gives at Shady Hill for selected undergraduates, who are almost stunned at impinging upon the consciousness of a man who had known Thackeray and Ruskin. Even if you do not aim as high as that, you can probably point out within a radius of six blocks from Harvard Square, in the "good" section of Cambridge, the houses of many of your professors, and though few work as hard at it as Copey or the Palmers, your chances of being entertained by some of them in the course of your college days are good.

You need some relaxation after these high-keyed social evenings with the faculty. You can play billiards at Leavitt and Peirce's— billiards is a gentleman's game, though you certainly ought not to be hanging around pool parlors. You can participate in dramatic performances in the new Harvard Stadium, including a pageant about Joan of Arc, with mammoth choruses to sop up all interested undergraduates. You can sing in the Glee Club. You *can* go to the Fogg Museum, which has been around since the mid-1890s, but the holdings are rather thin unless your heart leaps up at the sight of plaster casts. You can go out for the *Crimson* (briefly known as the *Magenta*!), or the *Lampoon*, or the *Advocate*, which is work but also fun—in fact, it is much to be feared that in every generation the contributors to the *Lampoon* get more laughs out of it than the readers. It was long before your time, but in view of what has become of him since, people are still talking about how William Randolph Hearst came to Harvard in the 80s and fitted out a sumptuous editorial sanctum for the *Lampoon* at his father's expense; but to show they could not be bought, the editors would not use it—then.

For some people in your class, and if you really are Frank Roosevelt, you're one of them, all these forms of escape from the daily grind are strictly minor. The big thing, without which everything else would be dust and ashes, is to get into "the clubs." Not just any clubs, *the* clubs for society types. The first thing, in your sophomore year, is to get into the Institute of 1770. The first 70 or 80 men elected to the Institute in any given year are automatically coopted into DKE, Dickey or the Deeks—they have accomplished the essential feat of "making the Dickey." If you get this far, then you probably join a "waiting club," and what you're waiting for is a "final" club—ideally, either A.D. or better still Porcellian, the apex of the social pyramid at Harvard. A minor revolution of falling expectations is, however, being enacted in your time as various waiting clubs cease to "wait" and brazenly declare themselves "final." You almost certainly aren't Frank Roosevelt or the equivalent and you don't even get into the tail end of the Institute—fewer than 20 percent of your classmates manage to squeeze in—and *he* didn't make Porcellian but had to settle for Fly. One of the minor mysteries of Harvard history is why A. Lawrence Lowell, of all people, didn't try to get into the clubs or failed to.

What difference does it all make? Everything. Or else, nothing. If you have any real prospects of getting in, or even unfounded anticipations, you probably care profoundly at every stage of the sifting. The archetypal tragedy in Harvard fiction of your time is to have the tastes and the money and the self-imputed flair to fit into the clubs but not to make it. As the fiction is always written from the vantage point of the clubs, this theme may chiefly reveal the unthinkableness of being left out for those who got in; but not entirely. The unsung form of Harvard heroism in these fictions is to say that one would rather be ignored at Harvard than taken up anywhere else. Harvard "indifference" is proverbial in your generation, and there is a kind of perverse accommodation and ultimate fidelity to Harvard in glorying in its exclusions even if you're the victim. But the beauty of the club system at Harvard is that if you have no chances and no illusions to begin with, you couldn't care less, though it is certainly borne in upon you that there are rich boys who look better and live better and dress better than you do and hang out exclusively with one another. But for poor boys that is part of a Harvard education too. If you are one of the outsiders at Harvard, you can affect to despise the insiders, but you don't.

For those who make it, club life opens many agreeable doors—you can begin to lead in Cambridge the kind of club life your father has told you about; and if you come from New York or Philadelphia or Baltimore or San Francisco, or some dubious place like that, you can safely be taken up by Boston society and introduced to the right sort of girls. There is a woman's annex in Cambridge, with a charter of its own since 1894, but Frank Roosevelt isn't going to meet his wife at Radcliffe, and one doesn't. Anyhow, the right kind of girl is finished, not educated. Her brothers are"fitted" for something, and the distinction is eloquent.

Boston is not restricted to those who get taken up by Beacon Hill. Anybody can run in (still by electric streetcars down to 1912) to Billy Park's for beer and Welsh rabbit—when Durgin arose in the land is unclear, but after your time. And there are other things for non-clubbies to do in Boston. When a Cambridge chippy is trying to break the ice, she asks if she hasn't seen you promenading on Washington Street on Saturday afternoon, and it could be. Not if you're a clubbie—at any rate, that is decidedly *infra dig.* for you.

Don't you do anything all of you together, rich and poor, preppie and non-preppie, clubbie and non-clubbie? Yes, the one bond that unites almost everybody except the intransigent aesthetes and the greasiest grinds is following the crew and, even more, rooting for the football team. You may be just in time for the glorious reign of Percy Haughton as football coach—he is going to build the teams that lick Yale 8 out of 12 games between 1908 and 1920. It is a sign of something that the only time in your undergraduate career that you and your classmates go slightly berserk is on the day of The Game. Professors William James and Walter B. Cannon think that you have found the moral equivalent of war. You are childishly hostile to Yale, and President Eliot is ashamed of you.

Procrastinate as you may, you really are going to have to take some courses and Eliot has complicated your life by leaving this up to you. You may have heard of a recent graduate named Sidney B. Fay who found that there was a professor lecturing on the top floor of Harvard Hall who shouted so loud that Fay could take complete notes from his window seat in Hollis, but fate seldom arranges your affairs as neatly as that. You *may* strike it lucky and have a chum that can cope with these things for you.

> Look here, Charlie. I can't make this thing out. It's all in a tangle. See here, I've got to fill up my hours some way or other;

you straighten this thing out for me. Find me some nice little course, two hours a week, say, that comes late in the morning, a good hour after breakfast; something easy, all lectures, no outside reading, nice instructor and all that?

What does Charlie come up with? or better still, what do you come up with if you roll your own? When Eliot put the wholesale elective system across in the 80s, many people expected and some feared that the next generation of undergraduates, more or less culminating in you, would flock to the natural sciences; but this has proved to be laughably wide of the mark. The fields that have gained at the expense of the classics and mathematics have been the social sciences (history, government, economics), modern literature (particularly English), and philosophy. You almost certainly do take a course with one or more of the never-to-be-equalled band of philosophers—William James, Josiah Royce, George Santayana, and George Herbert Palmer. By common consent, William James, now broaching the doctrine of pragmatism, is the greatest man on the faculty, an enchantingly informal lecturer sometimes distracted in mid-stream by his own thoughts and then striking his palm against his forehead and asking a man in the front row, "Now, what was I talking about?" He is by no means consistently incandescent, but when he strikes a spark, you never forget it. One of his chief tasks, after you have been bowled over by his lectures, is to discourage you from becoming a philosopher yourself. "Don't do it," he tells you unceremoniously, "you will be filling your belly with east wind."

The other philosopher who acquires liege-men for life is Josiah Royce, physically a kind of red-headed homunculus with a fetally disproportionate head and no neck to speak of, kindly but solemn, and much more respectful than James of conventional pieties. George Santayana has admirers but very few disciples. Everyone agrees that after a stumbling start, he has become one of the really great lecturers, but many people are chilled to the bone by his ironic detachment from all the doctrines he expounds, his total lack of his colleagues' moral earnestness.

The least distinguished of the philosophers, Palmer, gives the most popular course, Philosophy 4, on the history of ethics. Santayana, who studied with him as an undergraduate, despises Palmer—

"purring pussy Palmer," as Santayana's friend "Swelly" Bangs called him—but *you* presumably like being "levitated" far above all utilitarian ethical schemes and gently batted back and forth by what Santayana describes as Palmer's version of the Hegelian dialectic adapted to the purposes of a Sunday school.

In an overlapping field, you may well take Francis Greenwood Peabody's course in social ethics, familiarly known as "Drunks, Drains, and Divorce." A man who has recently come up fast as a student favorite is the professor of government A. Lawrence Lowell, whose highly characteristic formula in the classroom is, "Now what actually happens is this." In history, the great teacher is Albert Bushnell Hart, "Bushy" Hart, and bushy is the word for him, for he has an enormous unkempt handlebar mustache. You know (he takes care to see you do) that he was a classmate of Teddy Roosevelt and they still correspond. Bushy Hart always gives a rousing performance, reaches a tremendous conclusion exactly as the bell is ringing, and goes out to a storm of applause.

Your other great favorites are probably in literature. The elegantly dressed and disdainful Barrett Wendell, one of the Boston Wendells, with a high-pitched English accent that he brought back from an early trip abroad, teaches English and even American literature, though he says of the latter that it is "of little lasting potence." He boasts that his greatest service to America has been in combating coeducation at Harvard. You are not present, though he probably wouldn't care, when he has a memorable exchange with the young historian Roger Merriman.

> "In all the 25 years you have known me, Roger, have you
> ever heard me utter one liberal sentiment?"
> "Not one, sir."
> "Thank God."

When the eager undergraduate congratulated Wendell on his appointment as visiting professor at the Sorbonne and asked if Mrs. Wendell would be accompanying him to Paris, Wendell is supposed to have replied, "Young man, would you take a ham sandwich to a banquet?" Wendell's colleague, George Lyman Kittredge, the Shakespeare expert, is relished for his gigantic ego and impromptu wit, classically wrapped up together when he fell off the dais and said, "At last, I find myself on the level of my audience." The other great "character" on the Harvard faculty in your time is not particularly popular, though the consecrated few who take his courses think it is a matter of caviar to the general. Irving Babbitt, trained in Sanskrit, ostensibly teaches French, described in his own words as a "cheap and nasty substitute for Latin." In reality, Babbitt pursues his vendetta against Rousseau and permissiveness.

By no means all of the highly popular courses are soft options—Kittredge's certainly isn't—but cheer up, in times of peril, "the Widow Nolen" will take a motherly interest in your problems—William W. Nolen ('84), who runs the most famous of numerous cramming schools in the Square. For any of the big courses where the market is strong enough, he offers printed lecture notes, digests of the required reading, and forced feeding just before the examination. If you can pay the Widow's fees, you can escape from Harvard almost totally uneducated. Many do.

Among your classmates who take at least some of their work seriously, a high proportion feel that Harvard's main justification is to be "the college for writers." The teachers who arouse really passionate feelings, pro and con, are the ones that slave over your compositions or crack the whip over those that do—Dean Briggs in English 5, Copey in English 12, the otherwise forgotten Lewis E. Gates (briefly assisted by William Vaughn Moody) in English 22, George Pierce Baker in English 47, the unique Drama Workshop where you write, produce, and act your own plays. Some of these courses have severely limited enrollments, and you despair of getting in, but somebody has to win the draw. Copey, an assiduous self-publicizer, is better known in the outside world than Briggs, but the best Harvard writers prefer Briggs by a landslide (with a scattering of votes for Gates—Gertrude Stein took English 22, with Moody grading her themes, and so did Frank Norris, who conceived the germ of three of his novels as daily exercises for this course and dedicated *McTeague* to Gates). Those who either don't take Copey's course, or don't take *to* it, include VanWyck Brooks, T. S. Eliot, Conrad Aiken, John Dos Passos, and John P. Marquand. It is really only the budding journalists that admire Copey—but Walter Lippmann and John Reed are among them. It doesn't matter. If you amount to anything as a writer, nothing will persuade Copey that you didn't take his course and didn't like him. George Pierce Baker's 47 Workshop attracts all the aspiring playwrights, but as luck would have it, only two are going to be remembered in the history of the drama—T. S. Eliot and Eugene O'Neill (special student 1914–1915).

This, then, was Harvard in what is traditionally regarded as its golden age. Was there any prevalent tone or animus in the instruction in Eliot's time marking it off from other phases in Harvard's history? With the caution that no university is ever of a single piece, there was a remarkably candid embrace of advocacy on the part of many leading professors—in fact, the ones who were most popular. They were trying, more or less blatantly, to make converts to their own view of the world, seen as an instrumentality for giving direction to a student's entire life and defining his relationship to society. No doubt it was partly for this reason, as well as to allay any public apprehensions about the nakedness of their advocacy, that there was a surprising amount of recourse to adversary proceedings in the curriculum. The Democrat Henry Adams tried to create a foil for himself in the Republican Henry Cabot Lodge, and in later years Albert Bushnell Hart and Edward Channing were perceived, more subtly, as foils. The antithetical twins of the Philosophy Department, James and Royce, deliberately traded courses. Palmer filled in for Royce on the mutually acceptable understanding that he would do his best to root up "Royce's tender seedlings." But the point of these tremendously liberal proceedings was to legitimize advocacy. In Santayana's graphic metaphor, his colleagues in the Philosophy Department were glad to stock all kinds of shoes in their common shop window; but the object was to fit your own customer with the *right* shoes, all the better for letting him satisfy himself that the others wouldn't do.

Seen from the side of the people they ministered to, and the word will intrude itself, the legendary professors in Eliot's time were sages imparting wisdom for the conduct of life rather than mere information or objective reporting of the state of scholarship, and freely licensed to stray from their nominal subject-matter. They belong to the same genus as the lay prophets of Victorian England, John Ruskin, Thomas Carlyle, George Eliot, William Morris. By no accident, the man who was in many ways the role-model for the professorial sages at Harvard, Eliot's first cousin Charles Eliot Norton, lecturer on fine arts from 1874 to 1897, was Carlyle's and Ruskin's intimate friend and Ruskin's principal American disciple. Norton's famous course was entitled "the history of fine arts as related to society and general culture"—a highly Ruskinian formulation accurately conveying the almost boundless scope that Norton permitted himself. Wide-ranging pontification à la Norton was common in the first decade of the twentieth century, at a time when adversary proceedings were definitely on the wane. Men like Barrett Wendell and Irving Babbitt had no interest in fostering opposition to themselves.

The fundamental question remains whether the utterances of the sages of Harvard in the period from 1890 to 1914 had any prevailing drift. If the word "prevailing" is duly underscored, and the preeminence of William James discounted, yes. Much of the oracular instruction was Europocentric, particularly Anglophiliac, nostalgic, traditionalist, and elitist, and negatively defined by an aversion to the unbounded and unrestricted. It dwelt upon the meagerness of the American experience, called by Barrett Wendell the American "inexperience," and invoked the glamour of Western Europe and the aristocratic past. It was even wobbly in its Protestantism, perceived as the well-spring of the modern chaos.

All this could lead in two directions. It could and did lead to the abandonment of America by the one Harvard man of that generation who was destined to be read wherever English is known or translated. But it also led through Charles Eliot Norton to a clarion call for the young gentlemen of Harvard to save the United States from cultural and political dissolution. Though few in numbers, they might yet prevail by a narrow margin over the immigrant hordes and corrupt politicians. As the Boston (and Cambridge) Irish rose inexorably to power, it became natural to link these two perils. Three members of the class of 1889, including Charles Warren, became the bridge between the academic ruminations of Norton and the organized movement for the restriction of immigration. Barrett Wendell and A. B. Hart were also deeply influenced by Norton; and even Hart, after considerable hesitation, joined the ranks of the restrictionists.

Charles William Eliot was staunchly opposed to immigration restriction. The great irony of his régime was that Harvard produced in his last years almost a counter-culture and counter-ethos to his own. He was and remained till his death in 1926 a classic type of the American democrat, a believer in the winnowing of free men by harsh experience, but supremely confident of the continual improvement of the American republic and its unlimited capacity to assimilate new energies. This belief in the absorptive powers of a sound institution was undoubtedly bound up with his uncritical attitude toward the increase of numbers in Harvard College. Here, again, he was at loggerheads with the professorial sages who feared the unbounded and unrestrained and thought that a pullulating university could not be an ordered community answering to well-defined purposes—as, indeed, it could not, but that was no part of Eliot's ideal. In Santayana's words, discreetly echoed from many sides: "Harvard, in those the waning days of Eliot's administration, was getting out of hand. Instruction was every day more multifarious and more chaotic. . . ." Chaotic, multifarious, out of hand—all the qualities deplored by the counter-culture at Harvard were seen to be converging in Eliot's handiwork. He was no fool. He had a wry awareness of his vulnerability on this score, and winced a little with his enemies:

> I have supposed myself to have been pursuing certain educational ideals; but so many excellent persons have described the fruits of the past twenty-five years [written in 1894] as lands, buildings, collections, money and thousands of students, that I have sometimes feared that to the next generation I should appear as nothing but a successful Philistine.

He did not have to wait for the next generation. That was exactly what John Jay Chapman ('84) said about him on the morrow of his retirement from the presidency, when many people were offended by the crass but unctuous commercialism of the "Five-Foot Shelf."

Eliot had striven to apply the democratic tradition to Harvard College in the form of the wholesale elective system; but the students that he had set free to do as they saw fit flocked to the feet of men who deprecated America, disparaged democracy, and doubted progress. Eliot himself, by neglecting the problem of dormitories, had encouraged the well-to-do to hive off in cliques of their own and thereby contributed to undermining democratic attitudes in the College.

In this general setting, it is not surprising that the elective system itself came under fire. Admittedly, one did not have to have any philosophical animus against democracy to be shaken by the discovery that 55 percent of the class of 1898 had taken *nothing* but elementary courses. Professor A. Lawrence Lowell presided in 1903 over a faculty committee that took a highly critical view of what was happening to undergraduate instruction. President Lowell, in his inaugural address of 1909, spoke pointedly of "the extreme elective system" and said that the ideal in education was "a little of everything and something well." In 1910, effective with the class of 1914, the present philosophy of "concentration and distribution" for all students was imposed. As an attack upon the "pure" elective system, this was naturally very acceptable to many of President Eliot's critics, retrospecting upon their own time at Harvard.

> [Santayana] I began badly . . . in not having a fixed plan of study. President Eliot's elective system was then in the ascendant. We liked it, I liked it; it seemed to open a universal field to free individuality. But to be free and cultivate individuality one must first exist, one's nature must be functioning. What was I, what were my powers and my vocation? Before I discovered that, all freedom could be nothing but frivolity.

> [Babbitt's admirer T. S. Eliot in 1933] No one can become really educated without having pursued some study in which he took no interest—for it is a part of education to *learn to interest ourselves* in subjects for which we have no aptitude.

The concentration-and-distribution scheme, though highly welcome to many as a reaction against Charles William Eliot's permissiveness, merely served to strengthen in some faculty members a still deeper malaise about another and presumably irreparable aspect of Eliot's Harvard—his reform and encouragement of professional and graduate schools, and the increasing orientation of Harvard College (and all other colleges) toward the preparation of the young for professional training. "Concentration" need not look toward a profession, but in the circumstances, it probably would.

This development was peculiarly menacing to the sages of Harvard, for it seemed to be linked to a new conception of the professoriate that would leave no room for their own kind. The Harvard sages of the golden age saw the all-embracing tentacles of "the Ph.D. Octopus," William James's phrase, everywhere. Many of them were not Ph.D.'s—James himself, Wendell, Kittredge, Copeland, Babbitt—but this was not the real, or at any rate the sole, animus behind the most incisive critique of the new *régime*. Irving Babbitt saw in the Teutonized university a blind worship of science, or still worse a caricature of genuine science, that was steadily undermining the humanistic approach to literature that he championed and strove to exemplify. For "science" as applied to literature appeared to mean pedantic grubbing in philology and stubborn refusal to discuss the human bearings of literature. More than this, the spread of the scientific ideal to the study of history, henceforth to be known as social science, and to the study of psychology, deprived the humanistic approach to literature of its natural allies among the university disciplines and gave it the appearance of being the only one that could not invoke the sanctions of the blessed "science."

In this context, Babbitt protested bitterly against the dogma that nobody should be allowed to teach in a college without a Ph.D.

> But one may shine as a productive scholar, and yet have little or nothing of that humane insight and reflection that can alone give meaning to all subjects, and is especially appropriate in a college teacher. The work that leads to a doctor's degree is a constant temptation to sacrifice one's growth as a man to one's growth as a specialist. We must be men before being entomologists.

If, said Babbitt, instead of demanding original scholarship from a college teacher in, for example, literature, he was chosen for wide reading in the great books and the power to relate these to life, two advantages would follow—the undergraduate would get the instruction he needed to become fully human; and the modern heresy would be exploded that originality in research was the culminating ideal of life, with the corollary that mere assimilation of what was already known was contemptible. It was of a piece, Babbitt said, with "our small esteem for the 'ancient and permanent sense of mankind' as embodied in tradition, our prejudice in favor of young men and new ideas."

Babbitt objected to the elective system as permitting any callow youth to devise a program that entirely omitted the humanistic studies; but he thought it was far worse in Eliot to have created a situation in which the only plausible remedy for the evils of the elective system was to treat undergraduate instruction as a mere prelude to professional studies rather than as an end in itself. It was a doubly harsh verdict upon "the golden age at Harvard," but then, it was a product of that age.

OSCAR HANDLIN

A Small Community

Toward the end of the nineteenth century, Harvard education subtly changed. College remained an experience devoted to making men out of boys. But it no longer sought to do so by tight control; rather, it hoped to socialize the youths by giving them a stake in scholarship. The atmosphere of an enterprise devoted to advancing knowledge generated the respect of boys becoming men.

It is tempting to ascribe the change to the towering figure of Charles W. Eliot. And important he certainly was—for he ruled for full forty years, in addition to later service as a member of the Board of Overseers. Yet, though respected, he was not loved, and his success owed much to powerful external forces. Two binding elements established the link between scholarship and socialization: the promise that success in Harvard's four years would lead to future success in life; and immersion in a distinctive kind of collegiate community.

Harvard College offered no vocational or professional training. It led to no career; and no one attended for that reason alone in 1900 any more than in 1700. But in the last decades of the nineteenth century the generalized experience of college education acquired a

97

utility made visible in the change in models that influenced the careers of young men.

Business, politics, and the arts still remained open in the sense that various avenues of approach continued to provide access to any youth who sought achievement in those areas. But by the end of the nineteenth century, higher education tended to replace apprenticeship; and some careers demonstrated the utility of four years spent in Cambridge. J. P. Morgan, Jr., of the class of 1889, considered it worthwhile to earn a degree although his father, who established the firm, had not been a college man. Morgan, in time, found a place for Thomas W. Lamont (class of 1892), son of a Methodist minister who laboriously worked his way up in business. Theodore Roosevelt (class of 1880) elbowed his way ahead in New York politics and ultimately reached the White House; the stay at Harvard did not slow him. Boies Penrose (class of 1881) anticipated his own career as Pennsylvania's boss in a senior thesis that hailed Martin Van Buren as the greatest of American politicians. Precedents enough from the past showed Robert Frost and T. S. Eliot that they might gain as writers from attendance. College was not essential to such careers, but neither was it a needless detour, and associations established at Harvard might actually help.

In the professions of law, medicine, and teaching, the four-year college course became increasingly important as a preparation for life's work. In the last quarter of the nineteenth century, under the prodding of President Eliot and others, schools of law and medicine throughout the country struggled to raise their scholarly and scientific standards of instruction and began to demand a previously earned bachelor's degree as one of the credentials by which they admitted applicants.

Well into the twentieth century, the young man or woman without the appropriate collegiate qualifications could still find a place in diploma-granting institutions, which made no pretence to being graduate schools of law, medicine, or teaching. Indeed it long remained possible to enter such callings by testimonial and examination without formal schooling at all. But by the 1890s neither the lawyers nor the physicians any longer formed a uniform, undifferentiated group. A rapidly widening gap separated surgeons and other prestigious specialists affiliated with good hospitals from the neighborhood practitioner or rustic all-purpose horse-and-buggy healer, just as it did partners in firms that dealt in corporate and tax matters from the advocates in run-of-the-mill tort and criminal cases. Access to the desirable subgrouping was much narrower than to the profession at large, and it generally required completion of one of the good medical or law schools. Competition for places in those favored institutions mounted. No longer could anyone willing to pay the tuition be sure of admission. In that competition a Harvard degree was an asset.

The enormous expansion in the number of American teachers concealed a similar process of differentiation. The requirements for those posts varied enormously from state to state, indeed from county to county. A high school or normal school diploma often sufficed; and most schools of education, even those attached to universities, offered instruction at the undergraduate level. But in salary and status, a small minority of teachers in select private schools and colleges, standing quite apart from those who labored in public institutions, were products of Harvard and the other good universities.

At the end of the nineteenth century some youths still embarked upon their life's work through inheritance or purchase. Two very different journalists—William Randolph Hearst (class of 1886) and Oswald Garrison Villard (class of 1893)—thus acquired their respective publications, the San Francisco *Examiner* and the New York *Nation.* Harvard College provided no specific preparation for their careers any more than it did other students. Its bachelor's degree was not a credential for doing anything. Rare indeed was the young man who found vocational utility in a particular course or from a particular teacher. Repeatedly the faculty insisted, as did the alumni in retrospect, that the value of education there was vaguely general or liberal, that it derived not from specific books read or lectures attended but from shared experiences in the atmosphere of the place, which was in turn a product of the kind of community Cambridge was.

Cambridge was a large and growing manufacturing city. From about 2,000 in 1800, its population had risen to 52,000 in 1880 and 92,000 in 1900. Within it Harvard was a small, self-contained community, enjoying ties with the outer world but ruled by rituals and codes of its own. The contrast with Oxford impressed a visiting English don in 1893. He noted that the stranger whose walks did not lead through the Yard might live in Cambridge for some time without knowing he was in a university town. And teachers and students might pass an academic year without awareness of Lechmere or Cambridgeport. Again and again, its residents referred to Harvard's atmosphere, not precisely defined but pervasive and penetrating. The poet E. A. Robinson, coming in 1891 from Maine, understood that he had learned not from the courses taken, but from the environment that encompassed his life; later he wondered, more and more, just where he might have come out if he had never seen Harvard Square as he did.

The faculty, growing, no longer filled its ranks with New Englanders or with its own graduates; and it had no difficulty recruiting newcomers and holding their loyalty. The historian Frederick Jackson Turner scoffed at the idea that he might stay when he came as a visiting professor from Wisconsin; but stay he did—and not for the higher salary. There was no dearth of others who did the same. The German-born psychologist Hugo Münsterberg left the record of one such decision. He had already rejected an appointment at Oxford, when an invitation arrived offering him the chair at Königsberg. At the thought of the increase in remuneration, at the idea of going back to his "beloved Danzig home," above all at the prospect of becoming the successor of Kant, he immediately accepted. But the day after, "a long Sunday morning," as he sat and talked with Josiah Royce, he realized that here he would be among true friends his whole life long. He then decided that the break would cost too much and declined to leave. He thus followed the precedent earlier set by Swiss-born Louis Agassiz, who had rejected the profitable and prestige-laden offer to become director of the Jardin des Plantes in Paris. The attraction to Harvard was particularly significant in men not native to the place. But President Eliot frequently spoke with satisfaction of the number of professors "offered higher posts . . . carrying higher financial rewards" who had refused to leave because of "the perfect freedom of opinion" and "the deep respect of the community" they enjoyed.

Modest size nurtured an intimacy that held Harvard together. The teaching staff grew; the Faculty of Arts and Sciences in 1890 had numbered sixty members in all ranks and fifteen years later had swollen to one hundred and fifty, but was still not too large for familiarity.

None lived further from the Yard than three-quarters of a mile, a fifteen minute walk. And most professors of divinity, law, and medicine also had homes nearby.

George Santayana, one of the few to leave, criticized the little world of Cambridge because it lacked the cosmopolitan breadth of Paris or the night life of Madrid. It was the sort of place, he said, where two Harvard professors discussed whether it was well to serve "ice cream or salad, or any such pernicious luxury" in suppers for students. Such criticism was misguided or at least beside the point. Paris or Madrid it was not; but in this village within a city it was therefore possible to conduct a kind of decent social life, that, in retrospect, was and seemed to be extremely rewarding to those who participated in it.

Women played a role in that world not confined to whipping up suppers and presiding over their households. Their own family connections and wealth mattered; the fact that Mrs. Agassiz's maiden name was Elizabeth Cabot Cary added to her influence. Still she was an intellect in her own right, as was Mrs. George H. Palmer and many of their peers who had leisure to read, think, and act. With servants abundant and cheap, even the wives who lived on their husbands' salaries enjoyed disposable time. The ladies belonged to clubs of their own and maintained an information network more sensitive than that of the men.

Again and again, professors wrote of their delight in homes in which congenial spirits gathered, of informal shop clubs in which a man's "worth could be fully appreciated." The exuberant Münsterberg felt that he "had entered a truly spiritual community where the demand for high thinking and plain living was the life instinct." Even Santayana, who found little else to like about it, looked back to this feature of his stay in Cambridge with pleasure. Formal arrangements to bring the faculty together were unnecessary; the community itself generated sufficient gravity to keep its members from spinning apart.

Association with one another stimulated the scholars and also affected their teaching, which was not confined to the lecture platform or the laboratory. Liberated from parietal chores and from the drudgery of hearing recitations, knowing that the pupils in any given course were mostly there because they elected to be, the instructor could gladly teach, could indeed welcome the students in his home.

The younger and the older men were not equals but could treat one another with dignity and respect. The ease of contact with students at Harvard particularly impressed visiting lecturers like William Cunningham, who in 1900 came from the other Cambridge to teach economic history.

Harvard people knew little about the affairs of Central Square or Porter Square. But they did not feel isolated. As from the hub of the universe, significant connections radiating out from the Yard made them known at great distances, while informing them of events elsewhere. Ever more often, Harvard enjoyed the involvement of alumni, even of those who had not particularly relished their undergraduate years but who, returning at commencements or more frequently, felt a reawakening of ties they had not even known existed. Ralph Waldo Emerson (class of 1821)had not much cause, he sometimes thought, to wish his alma mater well. "I was not often flattered by success," he noted, "and was every day mortified by my own ill fate or ill conduct." Still, he mused, "when I went today to the ground where I had had the brightest thoughts of my little life and filled up the little measure of my knowledge, and had felt sentimental for a time, and poetical for a time, and had seen many fine faces, and traversed many fine walks, and enjoyed much pleasant, learned or friendly society—I felt a crowd of pleasant thoughts as I went posting about from place to place and room to chapel." Many other men caught glimpses, as he did, of the boys they had been, erased the memories of ancient resentments, began to serve and support the university, and supplied it with channels of communication to the wide world in which they lived and worked. Harvard clubs and alumni associations, dotting the country, created links to Cambridge.

Social and cultural lines stretched more directly to Boston, the self-denominated Athens of America. Trolley cars and later the subway connected Harvard Square with downtown, while livery stables provided vehicles for the students, identified by family or wealth, who enjoyed the hospitality of elegant homes on Beacon Hill or in Milton and Brookline. Some professors were familiar figures in the clubs that took pride in the intellectual interests as well as in the lineage of their members; and they and their wives participated in the activities of the Atheneum or the Fine Arts Museum or the Symphony, channels through which the influences of the wider world passed. In decades

Football form: "Passing the ball."

Baseball team, 1885.

Shooting club, 1886.

when high society sought its identity by the possession of culture rather than of mere money, Harvard associations had a worth, genuine though not precisely quantifiable. John Fiske (class of 1863), the most popular American historian of his day, was among those without formal University connections who chose to reside in Cambridge out of regard for those associations.

As it happened also, Boston was a focal point for publishing—not on New York's massive scale but in a focussed fashion that penetrated nationwide and molded tastes and opinions everywhere. No Pulitzers or Hearsts, no *Munsey's* or *Cosmopolitan* with their monstrous frenzied circulations; but the leisurely *Boston Transcript, Atlantic Monthly*, Little Brown, Houghton Mifflin, and Ginn carried words written in Cambridge and vicinity to schools and homes across the country—respectable, solid, weighty and influential.

The alumni and Boston were close to the Harvard hub. Other influences reached out to the whole nation and indeed across the Atlantic. Charles W. Eliot, for instance, linked the university to thousands of people who never came within reach of the Yard. His prestige as president lent weight to his views elsewhere; and his perceived power in American educational affairs reinforced his position at home. It became a matter of course that other institutions, through their own presidents and trustees, consulted him on appointments and on policies. As chairman of the National Education Association's Committee of Ten (1892), he helped formulate recommendations that shaped the curricula of high schools throughout the country; and he acted thereafter as spokesman for a wide range of reforms in secondary education. He was instrumental in creating the College Boards, a national system of entrance examinations through which Harvard and other universities drew upon a nationwide pool of potential students. On an even wider scale, his five-foot shelf of works from the whole world's literature defined the *Harvard Classics* (1910) as a canon for adult study and, by implication, made culture accessible to those who had never come to Cambridge. Eliot expressed himself freely and vigorously on social and political issues and, well after he left the presidency, continued to make his opinions known as a consultant and public figure. He identified Harvard with high culture; and through him ripples of the university's activities spread out in ever-widening circles.

Well-known professors also established networks of influence through their writings and their students. The History Department was not unique in that respect. The nineteenth-century instructors in that field had been amiable gentlemen, not unpopular as undergraduate teachers, but lacking in training and desultory in scholarship. Jared Sparks (class of 1815), having made a late start at his education, served as a Unitarian minister and editor of the *North American Review* before taking up the McLean professorship of history at the age of fifty. Henry W. Torrey had been admitted to the bar but never practiced and instead taught in a girls' school and at Boston Latin before coming to Harvard. Ephraim W. Gurney (who also gave courses in psychology) had also been a teacher in a secondary school; and Henry Cabot Lodge (class of 1871), like Sparks, had edited the *North American Review*. (Eliot was thus no great radical when he asked Henry Adams to work up medieval history.)

Their successors, a generation later, were Edward Channing (class of 1878), Albert Bushnell Hart (class of 1880), and Frederick Jackson Turner, each the product of graduate education in the new scientific history. Together they long set the national pattern for the teaching of American history, not only through their individual works, but also through Channing's textbook, *A Student's History of the United States* (1898), through Hart's *American Nation Series* (28 volumes, 1904–1918), through the collaborative *Harvard Guide to the Study and Teaching of American History* (1896), and through a corps of graduate students who went forth to staff departments throughout the country. Distinguished figures in other disciplines played similar roles. Their association with Harvard lent weight to their views, spurred the adoption of their books, gained positions for their protégés, and attracted young scholars to their seminars. Even the resentful criticism of former students like Vernon L. Parrington (class of 1893) was inverted recognition of Harvard preeminence. Meanwhile, national reputations and recognition by professional societies added to the status of the professorial luminaries in Cambridge. By the second decade of the twentieth century, some academic networks were international in range.

Stimulated by Eliot, new graduate schools created additional channels for the flow of Harvard influence. The university had long offered advanced instruction in divinity, law, and medicine. But soon after the young President took office in 1869, his reforms transformed those fields. In 1870 he appointed Christopher C. Langdell dean of law, initiated the modernization of teaching in medicine, and created distinctive degrees in divinity. Two years later the Graduate School of Arts and Sciences appeared and, in 1875, courses primarily for graduates. A year later the Museum of Comparative Zoology (founded in 1859) was incorporated into the university. The glass flowers arrived in 1887. The Fogg Art Museum in 1894, the Atkins Institution in 1900, the Semitic Museum in 1903, instruction in social work in 1906, the Harvard Forest in 1907, and graduate work at the Bussey Institution in 1908 added other dimensions to Harvard's offerings.

Intervention by a forceful individual, or local circumstances, or accident sometimes induced Eliot to act and dictated the timing, form, and function of a change. Still, the outcome, while not the product of a master plan, was also not merely a random aggregation of degree-granting faculties. No graduate school devoted itself simply to training practitioners, whether for the pulpit, the classroom, the courts, or the surgery. The unifying element in all of them, the purpose that established their professors as members of the Harvard community, was dedication to scholarship and the advancement of knowledge. The libraries, the laboratories, and the learned journals that were integral parts of the graduate faculties went far beyond the immediate pedagogical needs of the teachers, certainly beyond the immediate needs of all but a few students. The pervasive aura of scholarship even affected those ambitious only to use their degrees as keys to well-paying practices. In their dispersal across the country they too carried away a sense of having done more than master a craft, of having associated, however briefly, indirectly or painfully, with creative minds in the forefront of a discipline.

The Graduate School of Business Administration, founded in 1909, the final year of Eliot's administration, exemplified that president's attitude toward the place of professional education in the Harvard community. Business colleges had a long history in the United States, some as proprietary ventures, some connected with universities, some autonomous. Eliot had no desire to add to their number or to train managers in accounting and commercial practices. His was a larger view. The school was to offer graduate instruction to students who already possessed a first degree and it was to do so in the Yard, under the auspices of the Faculty of Arts and Sciences. (It was his successor who gave it autonomy and banished it to a gilded ghetto across the Charles.)

Eliot proceeded in this case as he had in the other graduate schools. He sought to do what had not been done before—to apply to business the scholarly techniques appropriate to advanced research and teaching. The man he chose as first dean and organizer, Professor Edwin F. Gay, continued to lecture in the Faculty of Arts and Sciences and trained a whole generation of economic historians who filled the professorships in that field in almost every great American university. But Gay did not limit his activity to the deanship or to teaching. Although in 1909 he rejected the post of Massachusetts Commissioner of Education, a year later he agreed to serve on the state's factory commission; and in 1911, as president of the American Association for Labor Legislation, he framed a model factory inspection act. Gay's profit-sharing plans also attracted attention. In 1914 he began to consult with the Rockefeller Foundation on the needs of the social sciences and he mediated labor disputes. In 1917, war took him to the nation's capital as adviser to the shipping and war trade boards and to a new Central Bureau of Planning and Statistics. Young Dean Acheson observed him there as "one of the kings of Washington."

The restoration of peace did not immediately bring Gay back to Cambridge. In 1919 he became editor of the *New York Evening Post*, which he staffed like a university department, with results that were intellectually distinguished but commercially disastrous. After four years he returned to Harvard, but until his retirement continued to serve as consultant to the United States Department of Commerce, to the National Bureau of Economic Research, to the Council on Foreign Affairs, to the *Encyclopedia of Social Sciences*, to *Foreign Affairs*, to the *Journal of Economic and Business History* and to the *Journal of Economic History*.

In the perspective of Gay's subsequent career, Eliot's choice seems not surprising. But in 1908, all those activities lay in the future. The more interesting question is—who was the man at the moment when the president selected him as dean?

Edwin F. Gay in 1908 had no experience with modern industry

and only an outsider's general knowledge of it. He was not a Harvard man, nor even a New Englander. Born in Detroit in 1867, he came to Cambridge in 1902 to teach medieval economic and agricultural history, invited for his scholarly qualifications and on the recommendation of Professor Charles Gross of the History Department, who had met him while they both did research in the Public Record Office in London. Gay had been influenced by John Dewey at the University of Michigan, then had studied with Gustav Schmoller in Berlin, where he wrote his dissertation, *Zur Geschichte der Einhegungen in England* (Altenburg, 1902), a sober study of enclosures. Through the busy years, he always hoped for time to revise and expand the thesis but never did, and often regretted the "distracted and dislocated career" that kept him from productive research. In Eliot's eyes he was an appropriate dean for the new business school not by virtue of later public service, but by virtue of his sixteenth-century scholarship.

Scholarship had a realm unto itself, residing in the Public Record Office and other archives, in libraries, in clinics, and in laboratories. Scholars did what they did there, out of concern with the sixteenth century or with medieval common law or with the use of bismuth as a contrast medium in x-rays. They required no justification for doing what they did. But by doing what they did for its own sake they also developed cultural attributes and knowledge widely applicable in the society in which they lived. And involvement in the same community with them enriched the students—even those without direct contact with them. Hence the university devoted its resources to libraries and laboratories which the undergraduates might or might not use but which their scholar-teachers required. The day was long since past when Franklin could fly his own kite or Dowse assemble his own library; research costs in every field climbed in the 1880s and 1890s, and even more so in the twentieth century. In other parts of the world, independent institutions largely supported by government bore those charges. It was immensely significant for the freedom of learning in the United States that Harvard absorbed those costs as part of the price the community paid for educating its youth. The burden of providing for the common enterprise of scholarship was one of the elements that bound the university together.

The pursuit of knowledge also guaranteed the University's excellence. The young men and their teachers quietly assumed that their Harvard was best—not only by virtue of its age, certainly not only for its wealth, but for its scholarship, however remote the share of any individual in it. President Eliot repeatedly warned that citizens in a democracy were vulnerable to quacks and charlatans. He wished the University to provide dependable guides to what was correct in art and literature, in economics and politics, in law and medicine, as in physics and chemistry. Since the students no longer formed a homogeneous body, their attitudes toward the University's culture and their involvement in it varied along a broad spectrum from cold indifference to passionate absorption, as status and motives for attendance dictated. But they could not react with hostility; loyalty to the institution demanded a belief in the excellence of the professors and the libraries and the museums, as of the football team or the *Crimson*. Not everyone in a pluralistic community participated in all of its activities; but the ten thousand men of Harvard had faith in the quality of whatever bore its name. The great achievement of Eliot's Harvard was to implicate a significant sector of American society in the support of its high culture.

Some students were aggressively anti-intellectual; others assigned to the pursuit of literature a higher worth than to the pursuit of wealth. One set of young men condescended to the other but accepted common membership in a single community. The tolerance of Dean LeBaron R. Briggs (class of 1875) assured Harvard places for them and others. William James (Harvard Medical School, 1869) lectured often about diversity, and his colleague in Philosophy, Professor Josiah Royce, as often lectured about loyalty, but the incident noted by Frank Norris (class of 1895) demonstrated that diversity and loyalty were compatible at Harvard. In November 1894, after another Yale football victory, the novelist came into breakfast and saw a Japanese whose countrymen had just taken Port Arthur. "I had no heart for life as yet; but *he* was on a winning side, *he* knew how it felt to be victorious, *he* triumphed. And as he read eagerly and thirstily his cheeks flaming with excitement I almost envied him . . . . 'Well,' said I as I pulled up my chair opposite him. 'It was a great struggle.'

He marked his place with his fork before looking up. 'Oh yes,' he answered, 'a great struggle. But if Fairchild had only kicked two inches further and two seconds sooner—fourteen to twelve, hey?' " Loyalty to the college transcended national differences.

Eliot's insistence on the utility of knowledge in a democracy spurred a growing number of students to use their learning for the general welfare. In the first decade of the twentieth century the university took pride in its role as nursery of independent thinkers. While William James noted that there was not a public abuse "for which some Harvard advocate may not be found," there were as many advocates in his day for reform; and the heady self-assurance of youths who believed themselves elect to transform the universe led to success in very different careers. More difficult to single out were the truly lonely and independent lads, infatuated with the suddenly discovered potentialities of the wide world of knowledge and avid only to drink it all up before the brief years elapsed. Thomas C. Wolfe (M.A. 1922) wanted to know everything on earth. At night, he prowled the Widener stacks, pulling volumes off the shelf, reading them like one possessed. The thought of this vast array of books drove him mad; the more he read, the greater seemed to be the immense, uncountable number he could never read. Not until later did such men think of what they would make of it all. For many, the Harvard involvement was more subtle and more penetrating than they knew in their student years. Dr. Alan Gregg (class of 1911), later director of medical sciences at the Rockefeller Foundation, long recalled something Professor Royce had said, something not really of intrinsic importance, except that Gregg had the strange conviction that here was something he did not in the least understand, but nonetheless something probably overwhelmingly important. He thought about it and thought it, and at long last understood it—at his fortieth reunion.

By the end of Eliot's administration Harvard had fused two elements in the culture it defined and transmitted: the inherited conception of a liberal gentlemanly education, now however available to students of every degree, had merged with that of scholarship, ever evolving as knowledge accumulated. Tradition yielded to science as the source of authority and, in Santayana's phrase, the professors became clergymen without churches.

The community devoted to that culture was small—small in the sense that it stood apart from the larger national community and held to standards of its own. In *American Notes* (1842), at the very start of the transformation, Charles Dickens, having visited Harvard, took inexpressible pleasure in observing the almost imperceptible but no less certain effect of this institution on Boston. He perceived at every turn the humanizing tastes and desires it engendered, the affectionate friendships it inspired, and the amount of vanity and prejudice it dispelled. "The golden calf they worship at Boston is a pigmy compared with the giant effigies set up in other parts of that vast counting-house which lies beyond the Atlantic; and the almighty dollars sink into something comparatively insignificant amidst a whole Pantheon of better gods." The visiting English novelist, repelled by the materialism and competitive individualism rampant in the expanding new nation, perceived an alternative force emanating from Harvard and also found a certain pathos in the desire of some Americans for something better for their sons. Whatever were the defects of universities in the United States, he wrote, they disseminated no prejudices, reared no bigots, and made no effort to dig up the buried ashes of old superstitions. They excluded no one because of religious opinions; and above all, the whole course of study and instruction recognized a world, and a broad one too, lying beyond the college walls. The community that emerged in the fifty years after his visit was a testament—living sentient evidence—of dedication to the values he noted.

Perhaps it was a rather perverse dedication to that evidence that accounted for President Eliot's espousal of poverty. He was prejudiced toward thrift—for the faculty. The mean salaries of 1902 ranged from $2,200 for assistant professors to $3,900 for full professors in addition to the $300 some of them earned by teaching at Radcliffe. Eliot's ascetic and devoted spirit required asceticism and devotion from the teachers of youth; and it mattered little, a hostile critic pointed out, if self-denial was prescribed by poverty instead of being elective. Eliot himself argued that the profession called for altruistic conceptions of life and duty. Whatever grievances troubled the teachers (or their wives) rarely surfaced, submerged as they were by the community's ideal of disinterested knowledge.

The editor, Ellery Sedgwick (class of 1894), asked: "What does a boy carry away from college?" And answered: a set of values. The boy had lived in a community free from the grosser inequities of the world, a society of scholars to whom learning was its own ample return, a republic where the crown of olives was the unmaterial reward. And if the young graduate was wise as well as knowledgeable, his diploma would tell him that in all this world there was no such reward as learning to understand. Much was rhetorical in such statements. But the rhetoric a community wished to hear about itself articulated the values it believed held it together and established its relationship to the wider world. In that happy first decade of the twentieth century, the university-college, one with itself, looked confidently back at its past and ahead to its future, secure in its own interpretation of the way it had come and of the way it expected to go.

Mutations in Eliot's University began to appear even before he left office; they spread at an accelerated pace thereafter. Almost imperceptibly, the smallness vanished. Cambridge grew in population until the 1930s. More important, the size of the student body increased. More important still, the number of men and women with faculty status soared, along with the staff and ancillary services they required. Eliot had firmly clutched control over finances and appointments; and his successors tried to do the same—unavailingly. Sheer size required administrators; bureaucrats appeared, and impersonality penetrated many levels of the institution's operation.

The commitment to diversity endured, but size complicated the ways of handling its consequences. In his *Annual Report* for 1900–1901, Eliot deplored the lack of loyalty and want of unity at Harvard, which he compared with other colleges whose members "move together as one man." He tended to blame the select clubs and sought an alternative to which everyone could belong. The alternative, the Harvard Union, already going up with the support of Major Henry Lee Higginson (class of 1855) and other alumni concerned with athletics, failed of its purpose. The magnificent building did not attract members with its billiard rooms, library, and easy chairs. The young men continued to retreat to the exclusiveness of their own clubs, so that within the decade firebrands like Lippmann and Reed launched attacks upon the aristocracy.

President Lowell's first effort to achieve unity uncovered other problems. He required all freshmen to live in elegant new dormitories along the river where common and dining rooms would perforce draw them together. The presence of a few black men, a sign of tolerance and a source of pride when everyone lived apart, now became an embarrassment. To exempt them from the general rule would be flagrant discrimination, to force them on southerners on terms of social equality, unthinkable. Lowell shrugged the problem off and launched upon the improbable effort to replicate the Oxford and Cambridge colleges in the house system, in blithe disregard of the insuperable differences between his own society and theirs. At Oxford and Cambridge the colleges were not all alike, for they selected their own members with due regard for regional and subject differences. Lowell wanted "men from different schools from different parts of the country, to mix together and find their natural affinities unfettered by the associations of early education, of locality and of wealth." That unrealizable aim also produced efforts at geographical and ethnic quotas in undergraduate admissions. The compatibility of diversity and loyalty that had impressed Frank Norris in 1895 grew more elusive with size, and efforts to impose it from above were fortunately futile. William James in 1903 had warned, "the day when Harvard shall stamp a hard and fast type of character upon her children, will be that of her downfall."

When Eliot took office in 1869 the faculty numbered twenty one. When he left office in 1909 it had expanded to 123. In 1963, it consisted of 452 permanent professors and associate professors and the count had risen to almost 700 twenty years later. The enlargement of the faculty reflected the twentieth-century transformation of knowledge; whole new fields of learning appeared and old ones developed in unexpected directions, all requiring specialization so that colleagues could hardly talk to one another outside the formal departmental structure. Shop clubs survived and, for a time, the senior common rooms of some houses provided a setting for interdisciplinary acquaintanceships. But collegiality waned and residence away from Cambridge ceased to be unthinkable. The flight to the suburbs that began in the 1920s accelerated after 1945 as real estate values rose and further diluted the sense of a small intimate community. Recurrent crises in the 1930s, 1950s, and 1960s exposed its fragility.

Alterations of scale also transformed Eliot's ideal of public service. Gay had been rather an exceptional figure and had resented distractions from his scholarship. He soon ceased to be alone in suffering drains of time in the service of good causes; Charles H. Haskins and Archibald C. Coolidge helped staff The Inquiry, Colonel House's desperate effort to prepare Woodrow Wilson for the 1918 peace negotiations. Demands for consultation increased in the 1920s and under the New Deal; and they swelled during the second world war, never thereafter to decline significantly. The burgeoning foundations, the increasing involvement of the federal government in financing research, and the utility of knowledge to business increased demands for faculty services. The peripatetic professor became a familiar figure, first on the overnight train and then on the jet.

Most of them remained faithful to their teaching obligations. They met their courses, set examinations, and served on committees. But they rationed time, now become a scarce commodity to be measured out in fractions, each with a cash value. Administrative duties became distracting burdens as did informal associations with students and colleagues. Leave became a perquisite rather than freedom for scholarship. Ever more often the professors jostled for space with worthy members of the university, who performed no teaching functions and had only a tenuous relationship to scholarship—journalists and labor leaders on leave, politicians out of office, important foreign leaders, and visitors to the proliferating research centers. The university also required the services of larger administrative and support staffs. The presence of the multitudes, evidence of the attractiveness of the university and of its service to the outer world, further diluted communal loyalties by dissolving the sense of intimacy associated with smallness, by injecting external worldly concerns and values, and by distorting the old focus on undergraduate education. Its three hundred and fiftieth anniversary finds Harvard as far from the university of 1900 as that was from the college of 1636. Yet something of the Puritan spirit had survived in Eliot's very different institution; and the cumulative heritage may still assert itself in the still more different university of the 1980s.

STEPHAN THERNSTROM

"Poor but Hopefull Scholars"

In the 1980s students are admitted to Harvard College without any reference whatever to their parents' ability to pay the costs of their education. Harvard is committed to meeting the financial needs, whatever they may be. In 1983–84 a staggering $18 million went to student aid, more than 15 percent of the total budget. Of that sum, $12 million was devoted to undergraduate assistance. Some 41 percent of those enrolled in the College received support, with the average grant running to $6,085, roughly half of the charges for tuition, fees, room, and board. It is difficult to imagine a college making a greater effort to ensure that its students are selected on the basis of ability alone.

It is only since the second world war that the College has been able to make admissions decisions without consideration of costs. But it always made some effort to open its doors to talented youths from families that lacked the resources to finance four expensive years in Cambridge. The character of these efforts over the centuries influenced the changing social composition of the Harvard student body at various points in history. Given the role that Harvard's products played in the life of the nation over this long span of years, an examination of the social origins of those who attended the College has more than antiquarian interest.

In the beginnings, Harvard College drew the bulk of its students from the upper ranks of society. The Great Migration of Puritans to New England included an impressive number of university men, most of them trained at old Cambridge. It is not surprising that this group of 130 graduates provided much of the initial leadership in the Bay Colony, nor that they sought to ensure that their sons had the benefit of attending the new college they erected in the wilderness only a few years after they arrived. More than half—fifty-five—of the first hundred graduates of Harvard were the sons of ministers or magistrates, occupations that placed their families firmly within the governing elite of the Bible Commonwealth.

The founders, though, did not regard higher education as a luxury properly reserved to the offspring of the affluent few. It was essential, in their view, to make Harvard accessible to "poor but hopefull Scholars whose parents are not able comfortably to maintain them." Strained though the College treasury usually was, public funds and donations from wealthy patrons like Lady Ann Radcliffe Mowson were used for scholarships that supported a quarter to a third of the undergraduates in the seventeenth and early eighteenth centuries. In 1710, for example, sixteen of the forty-nine students registered received assistance covering more than half the bill for tuition, room, and board, not counting the sums they earned for waiting on table and performing other chores.

During the eighteenth century, enrollments expanded substantially, from little more than fifty to three times that by the time of the Revolution. The supply of funds available to "poor but hopefull Scholars" did not keep pace with the growth in enrollment, however. The new donations and bequests were chiefly for books, buildings, or professors, not scholarships. In 1723 financial aid amounted to almost 12 percent of total student expenditures; by 1781 it had plunged to only 2 percent.

This relative decline in financial aid did not alter the social composition of the student body as much as might be thought, however, because in this era youths from humble backgrounds began to find another way of financing college—by working for years before matriculating to save enough money to pay their own way. Although direct evidence about the economic status of families whose sons went to Harvard is lacking, a revealing shift in the age profile of the student body took place in the latter half of the eighteenth century. In the 1750s only one out of eleven Harvard undergraduates delayed entry into college until he was at least twenty-one, presumably in order to accumulate a nest egg for his education; by the 1790s the proportion was up to almost one out of five. Eli Whitney, a poor farmer's son who had to teach school for several years before he was able to enter Yale in 1789 at the age of twenty-four, had many counterparts in late eighteenth-century Cambridge.

By every measure, the first half of the nineteenth century was a period of unprecedented growth and prosperity for Harvard. The number of College buildings grew from a mere half dozen to twenty, of endowed professorships from six to twenty-one. The College library tripled its holdings. Harvard's total assets rose from about $250,000 in 1800 to $1,250,000 at mid-century, three times those of Yale, five times those of Amherst and Williams combined. Financial contributions to the University averaged but $1,800 a year through the eighteenth century; by the second quarter of the nineteenth century donations were pouring in at a rate of almost $40,000 a year. It was extravagant to claim, as one young alumnus did in 1859, that "Harvard was the greatest university in all creation." But there was no doubt that by American standards its wealth and eminence were unrivalled. Although Harvard's emergence as a truly national university is conventionally located in the administration of Charles W. Eliot in the closing third of the century, giant strides in that direction were taken well before the Civil War.

In one respect, the character of the student body changed hardly at all in the course of these developments. At the end of the period as at its beginning, the undergraduate population was drawn overwhelmingly from New England and very largely from Massachusetts. Some 82 percent of the students enrolled in the College in the first decade of the nineteenth century were from the Bay State; in the 1830s the figure was 86 percent, in the 1840s it was 77 percent. That was rather greater geographical diversity than in the colonial period, to be sure; every single member of the classes of 1755, 1771, 1781, and 1793 had been from Massachusetts. But it hardly indicated that Harvard's catchment area was very broad. In the years 1800–1809, a mere 6 percent of the students came from outside New England, in the 1830s only 8 percent. The barriers to long-distance travel then were far greater than they would be later, but that was not the whole explanation. Yale was considerably more successful than Harvard in attracting students from the Midwest, and Princeton had much greater draw in the South. On this count, Harvard was a less national and more provincial institution in the antebellum years than some of the competition.

If the dominance of New England in general and Massachusetts in particular represented continuity with the past, a second characteristic of the antebellum undergraduate population was something new—it was overwhelmingly drawn from cities, especially the large cities and chiefly Boston, at a time when American society as a whole was still heavily rural. In writing about this period, Samuel Eliot Morison claimed that big city "swells" were "out-numbered by the horny-handed lads from country districts, 'fitted for college' and provided with a scholarship through the efforts of the local minister." According to him, there were "countless examples of that sort of Harvard student." When a count is actually made, though—an exercise he never attempted—the numbers turn out to have been modest indeed. In the 1840s, a bit more than half of the Massachusetts population and a large majority of the residents of the other New England states from which Harvard drew students lived either on farms or in small towns with fewer than 3,000 inhabitants. Only 5 percent of Harvard students came from such places. Almost two-thirds of them were from the Boston area, and most of the rest were from other large urban centers in the region. That "horny-handed lads from country districts" were such a rarity at Harvard was not a sign that these areas were too educationally backward to produce decent college material, for no less than 80 percent of Amherst and Williams undergraduates at mid-century came from such places. Harvard simply did not attract many students from rural and small town backgrounds.

Nor did it attract many students from families in the lower income brackets. The big city boys who increasingly predominated in

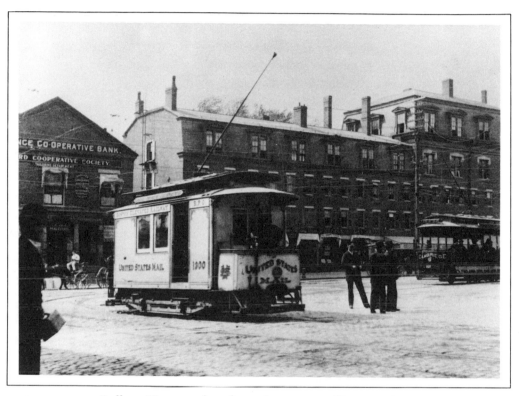

College House, taken from the corner of Dunster Street.

Entrance to the College Library (Gore Hall).

the college tended to come from quite well-to-do households. University spokemen were naturally inclined to deny that such a shift in the class backgrounds of the student body had occurred. Hence President Edward Everett's claim the "the majority" of Harvard students were "the sons of parents in moderate, narrow, and even straitened circumstances." He presented no supporting evidence, and it is doubtful that any could have been found. The costs of attending Harvard rose sharply in this period. Tuition was $20 in 1807, $75 in 1845, and $104 in 1860. With room, board, and other living expenses, a year at the College cost over $300 at mid-century, more than an ordinary laborer earned in a year and roughly twice the expense of Yale or Brown. Yet funds for student aid increased hardly at all. In 1831 only 34 undergraduates were receiving support at Harvard, as opposed to 144 at Yale.

The number of poor students who deferred their educations until they were able to pay their own way through school—the Eli Whitney types—also diminished in these years. The proportion of men who began their studies at the age of twenty-one or more dropped from 19 percent in the 1790s to a mere 6 percent by the 1850s. This did not reflect some general change in the larger society—for example, such general prosperity as to eliminate the need for many youths to work before college. Some 17 percent of Yale students in the decade before the Civil War enrolled at the age of twenty-one or later, and over 30 percent of men at such institutions as Brown, Dartmouth, Bowdoin, Amherst, and Williams. That the age range of the Harvard student body narrowed far more than at any other leading college indicated that the University was becoming a socially exclusive enclave populated largely by young men from affluent families from Boston and a few other New England cities.

Harvard certainly had more financial resources to devote to student aid than any of its rivals, had it chosen to do so. But the governing authorities did not seem particularly disturbed at the College's social transformation. Rising costs were met by tuition raises, with little thought to the problems of needy students who could not pay the toll. There were occasional expressions of concern. In 1826 a committee of the Board of Overseers declared that Harvard "was not designed by the founders to be an establishment for the rich alone," and went on to warn that "the yeomanry of our country and others of not large property" could no longer afford to send their sons to Cambridge. But another committee the next year scoffed at the idea that the University should "exhaust its resources for the support of a large number of indigent persons," and its voice was the one that was heeded. Such "indigent persons," the committee said condescendingly, "if not thus invited to the University, might become useful and respectable in some other course of life." It is revealing that the committee seemed unaware that, by then, pursuit of a "course of life" without higher education was not the only alternative for young men without the substantial wherewithal required to foot the bills at Harvard. A major reason for the foundation of new colleges like Amherst, Williams, Bowdoin, Colby, and Middlebury was precisely the wish to open up educational opportunities for students being priced out of Harvard. Professor Morison's "horny-handed lads from country districts" were largely to be found at schools like these.

Stiff costs and the paucity of financial aid were not the only things deterring otherwise qualified students from Harvard in the antebellum years. Religion also played a major role. Harvard went over to Unitarianism early in the century, on the eve of the great outburst of evangelical zeal known as the Second Great Awakening. More than any other American college it was noted for its tolerant, cosmopolitan atmosphere. Thus the striking fact that three of its fourteen instructors and administrators in 1831 were Roman Catholics, at a time when most American Protestants regarded Catholics as agents of the devil. However commendable, such intellectual openness appeared to be religious indifference, even "godlessness," to those who had given their hearts to Jesus in the revivals. Revivalist passions were stronger in the West and South than in the Northeast, and more powerful in small towns and rural areas than in the big cities, a fact that helped to skew the composition of the Harvard student body. Charles Franklin Thwing's 1897 study of living alumni of Harvard and Yale attributed Yale's much stronger following in the West to its safely orthodox Christian image. To many in the West, the author remarked, "the word 'Unitarian' means something almost as harrowing as the word 'Indian' meant . . . forty years ago." Not only were Yale, Princeton, Dartmouth, Amherst, and Williams more affordable than Harvard; they embodied an evangelical piety and purity much less in evidence in Cambridge.

Striking evidence of the distinctiveness of antebellum Harvard in this respect is visible in the career paths followed by graduates of various colleges in the half century after 1825. Although new scientific and technical occupations expanded rapidly as a result of industrialization, the ministry remained the single most frequently chosen profession for educated men in this period. No less than 24 percent of Yale and Dartmouth graduates, a third of those from Williams, 43 percent of those from Middlebury, and 46 percent of the students from Amherst became clergymen. Harvard stood out as by far the most secular of America's colleges, with only 11 percent of its alumni entering the ministry. Harvard's aloofness from the spirit of an evangelical age, its advanced willingness to tolerate all shades of religious persuasion, distinctly limited its appeal in those sections of the country and among those social groups that adhered most firmly to Protestant orthodoxy.

Before the Civil War, as George Santayana later put it, Harvard was largely "a seminary and academy for the inner circle of Bostonians." After the turn of the century, the character of the student body had changed to an almost unrecognizable degree. John Reed (class of 1910) noted that "all sorts of strange characters of every race and mind, poets, philosophers, cranks of every twist were in our class . . . No matter what you were or what you did—at Harvard you could find your kind." Perhaps this statement displayed something of the romantic enthusiasm Reed soon was to show towards the Bolshevik Revolution. But a thoughtful contemporary survey of *Great American Universities* yielded a similar verdict. The author singled out Harvard not only for the eminence of its faculty and the extraordinary range of its course offerings, but for the exceptional diversity of its student body. "The ideal of Princeton is homogeneity," he concluded; that of Harvard diversity. "The Harvard students are gathered from all over the world, admitted under all sorts of conditions, and given the most diversified training." Princeton, by contrast, offered "one particular kind of college training to one rather limited social class of the United States," a comment that could have been applied with some justice to Harvard itself half a century earlier.

One element of Harvard's new diversity was geographic. President Eliot strongly believed that it was "for the safety of Harvard College, and for the welfare of the country, that the College draw its material not from Massachusetts or from New England alone; but from the whole country, and that the graduates of the College spread themselves over the whole country." In the four decades of his administration, 1869–1909, Harvard's outreach grew notably. The proportion of students from the Bay State, always at least 70 and often over 80 percent of antebellum classes, fell to about half by the turn of the century. (It was down to 18 percent in the class of 1986.) Men from other regions of the country accounted for 37 percent by 1890 and 42 percent in 1905. The sons of proper Bostonians still went to Harvard more often than not, but they were no longer the dominant element in the College.

As significant as this broadening of the geographic base of the College was the sharp rise in the proportion of students who entered Harvard without costly preparation in a private secondary school or by a private tutor. Only a third of Harvard undergraduates in the 1860s were the products of public schools; two-thirds had attended Andover, Exeter, or other preparatory schools, or had been tutored at home. By the early twentieth century, the proportion of youths from private schools had fallen to 47 percent. Although the change reflected the upgrading of public secondary education in the years since the Civil War, Harvard's traditional rivals were much slower to tap this new source of talent. "Preppies" still made up over two-thirds of the student body at Yale and more than three-quarters at Princeton when they had become a minority at Harvard. In its welcome of students from public schools, Harvard became distinctly the most democratic of the "Big Three" schools.

A full explanation of the College's growing success in attracting students from Minnesota and Mississippi as well as from Massachusetts, from Peoria High School as well as from Phillips Academy, would have to note the influence of the waning of the evangelical passions that had deterred many young men from coming to Cambridge earlier in the century, the appeal of the elective system, the abolition of compulsory chapel, and other student freedoms introduced under the Eliot regime. But the principal influences were the decline in the relative expense of Harvard compared to other colleges and the development of a far more generous scholarship program. By

John Lovett—"John the Orangeman"—native of County Kerry,
associated with the College for a full half-century, mascot of all athletic
contests, and ex officio *member of every Harvard team.*

Contemplating mortality, 1889.

1870 tuition was up to $150, the highest in the country; but it remained there for the next forty-five years, while other institutions increased their charges. An 1878 report on *American Colleges: Their Students and Work* found Harvard more expensive than any other college except Columbia, with a rock-bottom minimum annual student expenditure of $450. But the minimum for Yale was $400, for Amherst, Brown, and Princeton $350. The enormous disparity that had prevailed earlier between the costs of Harvard and other outstanding colleges had shrunk considerably, and it continued to do so later in the century.

What is more, by 1878 Harvard had by far the best-funded scholarship program in the nation. The author of *American Colleges* remarked, "to a poor man of brains Harvard may be the cheapest college, as its scholarship and other funds may pay his entire expenses." Harvard's renewed interest in helping out "poor but hopefull scholars" began in 1852, when the Alumni Association asked each class to raise funds to endow a scholarship in the College. This campaign soon began to bear fruit, and several individual donors made sizable bequests for the same purpose. In the late 1870s Harvard each year provided 112 grants to undergraduates, about a seventh of those enrolled. The average amount was $235 annually. Another $3,500 was distributed in loans, for a total of almost $30,000 in aid annually. Yale then offered only twenty-eight regular scholarships, at an average of $60 each, for a total of only $1,680, with another $12,000 a year reserved for prospective ministers. Amherst, Brown, and Dartmouth, with 101, 100, and 124 scholarships respectively, rivalled Harvard in the number of students aided; but the average grant ranged from $70 to $86, only a third as much as at Harvard. Princeton offered an unspecified but "limited" number of scholarships worth $75. For youths who required aid, Harvard's much larger financial awards more than made up for its higher costs.

President Eliot had some misgivings about the growth of the scholarship program. He worried that dependence upon aid was corrupting, and in 1876 warned darkly that "the Communist doctrine that it is the duty of the community to provide every child gratuitously with the best education he is capable of receiving has obtained a certain currency in late years." But his deep commitment to meritocratic principles of selection, to finding the best qualified students regardless of their parents' ability to support them, outweighed those fears. In an often-quoted 1904 letter he summarized his differences with his persistent critic, Charles Francis Adams, Jr. Adams, he claimed, "wanted the College to be open to young men who had either money or brains." Eliot insisted instead that it should be "open equally to men with much money, little money, or no money at all, provided they all have brains." In the antebellum years, when Eliot himself was an undergraduate (class of 1853), Harvard had very few students with "no money at all." During Eliot's presidency, and since, the University has devoted substantial resources to realizing that aim, and has benefited from the diversity the effort made possible.

Even though Harvard had the most extensive scholarship program in the nation, its student body remained predominantly middle class, even upper middle class, in origin. In the early 1870s, half the students in Cambridge could afford a personal servant and 84 percent had fathers who were professionals or businessmen. Only 4 percent were the sons of farmers (a group that comprised half the nation's labor force), and a mere 7 percent were the children of manual laborers (another very large group). Thirty years later, despite the pronounced rise in the proportion of students from public secondary schools, the distribution of parental occupations was identical. Between 1870–1875 and 1903 the size of the various occupational categories changed by hardly a percentage point (see table).

It is tempting but erroneous to interpret these figures as evidence of the gross inadequacy of scholarship assistance in the Eliot years. Differences in parental wealth, it might seem, were responsible for the highly unrepresentative class backgrounds of Harvard students. There is no certain way of telling whether many poor but extremely able scholars turned away from Harvard for want of more scholarship funds. But it is instructive to consider these results against two other points of reference. Although tuition at the University of Michigan was free for residents, and other costs were well below those at Eastern private colleges, a mere 6 percent of the students at Ann Arbor in 1902 were from blue collar homes, actually a shade below—though, to be sure, not significantly below—the proportion at Harvard.

It is even more illuminating to compare the social composition of the Harvard student body in the 1870s and 1903 with that of 1984,

Occupational Distribution of the Fathers of
Harvard Students, 1870–1986 (in percentages)

Occupations of fathers	Students enrolled, 1870–1875	Students enrolled, 1903	Students, class of 1986
Professionals	28.6	29.5	59.3
Businessmen	55.7	56.7	31.0
Government workers	4.2	3.0	4.3
Farmers	4.2	3.0	0.5
Manual workers	7.3	7.8	5.0

when poverty *per se*—as opposed to various disabilities associated with family poverty—does not bar any applicant from the college. With over 40 percent of the undergraduates on scholarship in 1984, sheer lack of funds cannot be a major deterrent keeping anyone from attending Harvard. Yet the offspring of professionals and business-men form an even more overwhelming majority of the class of 1986 than they did in the 1870s or 1903, though it is now those from pro-fessional families who predominate, a dramatic shift. The children of farmers or blue collar workers, 11 to 12 percent of the student body earlier, currently comprise little more than 5 percent of the under-graduates. The sons and daughters of doctors and dentists alone out-number them by three to one in the class of 1986 (15.7 percent of the total), although there are 112 times as many manual laborers and farmers as doctors and dentists in the general population. The chil-dren of college professors, almost 14 percent of the class of 1986, and of attorneys (9.8 percent), are likewise immensely overrepresented in comparison with their tiny share in the labor force as a whole.

Yet current admissions policies are far from biased against chil-dren of working class, farm, or lower middle class origins. The expla-nation for their relative absence is uncertain, but it is evident that neither the desire to expose oneself to the pressures of an academic environment like Harvard's nor the traits necessary to surmount the admissions barriers are randomly distributed in the population. Even when direct financial deterrents to attending such an institution are removed, as they have been, growing up in a particular kind of family powerfully influences both the aspirations and the academic abilities of youths. This was undoubtedly true seventy-five or one hundred years ago as well. Although Harvard sought a socially diverse student body, the range of variation in the economic status of the parents of its students was necessarily rather limited.

Be the herald of Light and the bearer of Love,
Till the stock of the Puritan die.

The closing lines of "Fair Harvard," written for the Bicentennial Celebration of 1836, suggested that the College was an extension of the Society of Mayflower Descendants, and that its future depended upon the continuing ascendancy of the descendants of the first settlers of New England. The complexion of the antebellum student body was in accord with that insular vision. After the Civil War, under the leadership of that quintessential Puritan, Charles W. Eliot, Harvard developed a degree of ethnic and religious diversity that appalled exponents of the "Fair Harvard" ideal. The shift towards cosmopolitanism met resistance and suffered some serious setbacks in the 1920s during the administration of A. Lawrence Lowell. But its long-term success was essential to Harvard's continued greatness.

Although it did not provide a precise measure of the strength of the Puritan element, an 1870 survey of student religious preference revealed considerable homogeneity. Almost 80 percent of the 563 undergraduates responding adhered to one of the three faiths that were then in favor with the Yankee upper class—Unitarianism, Episcopalianism, or Congregationalism. Almost a fifth belonged to other Protestant sects, and there were but seven Roman Catholics and three Jews. The small numbers of the latter two groups is not surprising. There were as yet only a handful of Jews in the United States. The Catholic population was already fairly substantial, particularly in Boston, but the great majority were impoverished Irish immigrants who could not afford to keep their children out of the job market to finish high school, much less to attend college. The few who were in a position to enter higher education were strongly encouraged by their priests to remain safely within the fold by attending Catholic institutions. That there were in the College no black students at all was also not surprising, given the poverty and illiteracy of the Afro-American population and its overwhelming concentration in the South.

The black presence at Harvard remained almost invisible throughout the late nineteenth and early twentieth centuries. As a graduate student, W. E. B. Du Bois was a commencement orator in 1890, and another black was named class orator the same year after winning the Boylston Oratorical Contest. But only 160 Afro-Americans studied in the College before 1940, most of them after 1890. In the Eliot years blacks were as well treated at Harvard as at any elite college. President Lowell, on the other hand, was worried about unwise "social commingling," and barred blacks from the dormitories until public opposition made him reverse course in 1923. The shift was partial and grudging; black students were segregated from whites in College residences until World War II. The main force depressing black enrollment, however, was not a sense that Harvard was unwelcoming but the absence of a sizable pool of black students who could meet the admissions requirements, a situation which changed only as a result of the remarkable economic and educational advances made by blacks after World War II.

Other groups found many more doors open to them in the larger society than did blacks, and as they experienced upward social mobility they began to send young men to Harvard. Thus the proportion of Catholics in the student body, most of them the American-born children of immigrants, edged up from 1 percent in 1870 to 4 percent in 1881 and 9 percent in 1908. The integration of a substantial Catholic minority provoked very little unease and tension.

The same cannot be said of the Jews. Although they were a much smaller element of the population than Catholics, exceptional economic mobility and zeal for learning led them to outnumber Catholics at Harvard by World War I and convinced some that the university had a serious "Jewish problem." Only 1 percent of the student body in 1881 was Jewish; in 1908 it was 7 percent, in 1918, 10 percent, and in the freshman class that entered in 1922, almost 22 percent. Xenophobic fears of the "new immigrants" in general had been rising in the land since the 1890s, culminating in the racially restrictive immigration laws of 1917, 1921, and 1924. In many quarters Jews were viewed as the most pernicious of all the new immigrants—clannish, crass, pushy, and amoral. Antisemitism was at an all-time peak in the United States in the 1920s, and Harvard was not unaffected. In 1922 President Lowell publicly called for a limit on "the proportion of Jews at the college," on the grounds that their rising numbers were responsible for the growth of "anti-Semitic feeling among the students."

The scheme was sharply attacked in the national press and was rejected by a special faculty committee appointed to advise the Board of Overseers and by the Overseers. But if Lowell was formally rebuffed, and Harvard remained officially committed to providing "equal opportunity to all, regardless of race and religion," the advocates of exclusion won a veiled victory. The controversy ended with the adoption of a new admissions system, one that relaxed standards for students outside the Northeast to obtain a better "regional balance" in the College. The idea of making special allowance for deficiencies in the preparation of students from the less developed regions of the country seemed just, and was in accord with President Eliot's dream of giving Harvard a strong constituency throughout the nation. But in fact the scheme was not implemented in a way that created more places for Southerners and Westerners by turning away marginal candidates from P.S. 134 and Choate alike. As it turned out, the necessary space was created by cutting admissions from the big city public schools, and it was hardly coincidental that many of these rejects were Jewish. By the close of Lowell's administration in 1933, the proportion of Jewish undergraduates had fallen to about 10 percent.

That was still high by comparison with the other Ivy League schools, and it began to climb again after James Bryant Conant took office. Even in 1930, with the results of the new admission system plain to see, a study of antisemitism in American universities rated Harvard considerably better than Yale, Princeton, Columbia, Cornell, Johns Hopkins, and Northwestern. Nevertheless, the attempt to impose an open Jewish quota and the adoption of an admissions scheme that had much the same effect should be recalled as a corrective to the self-congratulatory rhetoric that is the staple of most anniversary celebrations.

Harvard's reputation for diversity, tolerance, and pluralism rested upon solid foundations. But its record was by no means unblemished. The University's treatment of students from varying social classes and ethnic backgrounds reflected its image of itself and society. Changes in that image were revealed in changes in whom Harvard chose to welcome into "the fellowship of educated men."

OSCAR HANDLIN

Epilogue—
Continuities

The celebrations that punctuated Harvard's history were occasions both for contemplation of the future and for reflections on the past; always the participants concluded that while much had changed, as much had not. And the alumni and others who mark the 350th anniversary in 1986 will probably look back at the tercentenary of Conant's Harvard in 1936 with a shock—how much is new, how much is not. Just so those who attended in 1936 looked back at Eliot's Harvard of 1886.

The century since 1886 wrought great changes in the University, but a permanent core survived.

The changes, the easier to describe, manifested themselves most dramatically in an alteration of scale. In 1886 the University formed a small community focused on the Yard, and it still retained that character in 1936. In the latter year, it had already planted outposts in Soldiers Field and in Boston, as well as in more distant settings in Cuba and Africa. But the buildings were essentially those of the early part of the century, although the Houses had crept down toward the river.

The outburst of building after 1945 continued to alter the landscape—and not only with sober Georgian or Victorian structures.

Cambridge and the medical area in Boston housed a veritable museum of modern architecture, appropriate to the novel activities within them. The number of students grew, as did the size of faculties, and both increases mirrored the complexity of a university that offered instruction and performed research in many fields.

The Tercentenary Theater of 1936 symbolized the unity that rested on the assumption of common goals and interests. It was taken for granted that the whole body of participants, that is, all the members of the community and their guests, would fit into the space between Memorial Church and the Widener Library, the two structures that expressed the unifying goals of the University—piety and learning. It is hard to conceive of any analogy in 1986. Even Commencements that drew graduating students together were more likely in the 1980s to display differences than expose similarities.

Teachers and students in this decade are no longer the only members of the University. A vast array of others has joined them, as the institution changed. These people are immersed in scholarship to varying degrees—they include librarians, curators of museums, editors, and technicians; and in addition, a growing administrative bureaucracy. An expanding staff services these activities, maintains the facilities, and keeps the operations on a sound fiscal basis. Indeed, it becomes ever less possibe to conceive of Harvard as a single institution, although it has remained far from the multiversity characteristic of other parts of the country. The earlier tendency toward diversity in the student body continues; a particularly determined effort was and is made to increase the representation of all the racial, ethnic, and social elements in the American population, whatever that takes in the way of scholarship support. In the process, Harvard has gone a long way toward becoming more a national and less a regional institution.

Tuition declined steadily as a percentage of University income; although charges rose rapidly, expenses increased even more swiftly. The University's endowment grew as a result of prudent management and the continued generosity of alumni and other donors. But although income from that source rose in absolute terms, it did not stretch enough to sustain the ballooning expenses. Increasingly therefore, Harvard, like other institutions, turned to outside sources for support, and particularly to grants from governments as well as foundations. Dependence on such soft money left the individual scholar vulnerable to pressures far different from those that operated in an earlier, simpler period.

Often the University in the 1980s has been on the defensive, as if it could no longer take its existence for granted, as if its activities were not valuable in themselves but required justification by social utility. The compulsion to prove that Harvard did good has been more than a device to elicit financial support; it expresses a genuine concern that a troubled universe can no longer afford the luxury of pursuits confined to an ivory tower, so that scholarship has to prove its worth not on its own terms but by service to the nation and the world.

Locally, too, the University has been on the defensive. Cambridge is no more hospitable a community than it had been for a century past, although Harvard and M.I.T. have contributed essential strength to the economy of the city and of the region, to say nothing of the worth of their cultural and scientific achievements to the nation and to humanity. But growth left Harvard a vulnerable giant, exposed to the petty stings of demagogic politicians, insensitive to its importance, but keenly sensitive to the pressures its size puts on the city.

Nevertheless, continuities persist. The worldwide recognition of Harvard's greatness already marked in Conant's years, indeed even in Eliot's years, has survived; and that recognition rests on the fruits of scholarship. For whatever concerns occupied the changing generations through the passing centuries, the concern with learning did not wither. Other interests waxed and waned; this sometimes blazed, sometimes flickered, but endured.

Here in the wilderness the first founders planted an institution that grew in ways they could not have anticipated. That poor pilgrim people, their estates much wasted, in erecting a College sought to make the whole world understand that spiritual learning was the thing they chiefly desired. They would not have felt themselves total strangers in the University 350 years later.

The Natural History Society, 1871.

Some Notable Harvard Students
chosen by Donald Fleming

The following list contains the names of slightly more than 700 persons who attended Harvard or Radcliffe College or one of the Harvard professional schools. Perhaps 75 of them are known to the vast majority of educated Americans. Almost all of those listed performed admirable labors of one sort or another, but the solid mass of virtue has been leavened by a handful of memorably despicable people. The criterion for inclusion was to have achieved celebrity, retrospective or contemporary and preferably enduring, or to have left some identifiable mark upon the world. Certain categories have been automatically included—Signers of the Declaration of Independence, Presidents and Vice-Presidents of the United States and major nominees for both offices, members of the United States Supreme Court, members of the President's Cabinet, heads of principal American diplomatic missions (to Britain, France, Prussia/Germany, Italy, Russia, Japan), and Nobel prizewinners. Apart from these inclusions, the list is a frankly personal selection by the compiler, though intended as far as possible to incorporate estimates that would be widely shared by competent judges in the relevant fields of endeavor. No pretense is made that *only* these persons achieved celebrity or distinction. Equally deserving names must have been inadvertently omitted and others misguidedly excluded. The list of Harvard students has been supplemented by a small selection of notable faculty (and staff) members who had no earned Harvard degrees. Neither list has any official standing whatever.

Anyone who took a bachelor's degree at Harvard or Radcliffe is listed without further explanation by the year of receipt. Persons who matriculated for a Harvard or Radcliffe degree but did not receive it are listed by the last year in which they were in residence and the total period of residence is specified. The same principle applies to "special," i.e., non-matriculating, students. When Harvard or Radcliffe graduates took, or matriculated for, *further* Harvard degrees (with one exception stated below), this information is supplied in *square brackets*. Subject to the same exception, people whose undergraduate careers were elsewhere are listed by the year of receipt of their first advanced Harvard degree (or last year of matriculation toward this degree), with a stipulation of the degree or faculty in question. If such persons proceeded to *further* advanced degrees at Harvard, this is indicated in square brackets. The sole exception to the specification of advanced Harvard degrees is that all reference to the Harvard AM is suppressed for anybody who proceeded to the Harvard PhD.

1642   [Sir] George Downing [Downing Street]
1646   George Stirk(e) or Starkey [alchemist]
1649   Urian Oakes [pres. HC]
1650   Leonard Hoar [pres. HC]
1651   Michael Wigglesworth
1656   Increase Mather
1657   Elisha Cooke I
1659   Samuel Willard [act. pres. HC]
1662   Solomon Stoddard; Benjamin Tompson [poet]
1665   Joseph Dudley
1668   Abraham Pierson [1st rector Yale]
1670   Nathaniel Higginson [mayor Madras]
1671   Samuel Sewall [diarist]; Edward Taylor
1673   John Wise
1676   Thomas Brattle
1678   Cotton Mather
1680   John Leverett
1681   James Pierpont
1684   Gurdon Saltonstall [gov. Conn.]
1690   Paul Dudley; Benjamin Wadsworth
1692   Benjamin Colman
1693   Henry Flynt ["Tutor" Flynt]
1695   Jonathan Law [gov. Conn.]

1697 Elisha Cooke II; John Read
1699 Jonathan Belcher I; Jeremiah Dummer
1701 Timothy Cutler; John Stoddard
1705 Edward Holyoke [pres. HC]
1707 Thomas Prince
1708 Thomas Robie
1710 Edward Wigglesworth I
1711 Thomas Cushing I; Elisha Williams
1714 Ebenezer Gay
1715 Benning Wentworth
1721 Charles Chauncy; Isaac Greenwood
1724 Andrew Oliver
1725 Mather Byles; Timothy Walker
1727 Thomas Hutchinson; Israel Williams; Jonathan Trumbull I
1728 Jonathan Belcher II; Josiah Quincy I
1729 William Williams [Cont. Congr.]
1730 Peter Oliver
1732 [Professor] John Winthrop; Timothy Ruggles
1735 Samuel Curwen; John Phillips [Exeter Academy]; Meschech Weare [pres. NH]
1737 Andrew Eliot
1740 Samuel Adams; Samuel Langdon [pres. HC]
1743 Samuel Cooper; James Otis
1744 Thomas Cushing II; Jonathan Mayhew
1745 James Bowdoin I [gov. Mass.]; [General] James Warren
1746 [Dr] Edward Augustus Holyoke
1747 William Ellery
1748 [General] Artemas Ward
1749 Gideon Hawley; Robert Treat Paine [Signer]; Edward Wigglesworth
1751 William Cushing [US Supr. Ct]; William Williams [Signer]
1753 Thomas Oliver; Oliver Wendell
1754 Benjamin Church [Traitor]; John Hancock
1755 John Adams; Jacob Bailey; William Browne [gov. Bermuda]; Samuel Locke [pres. HC]; [Sir] John Wentworth
1759 Jonathan Trumbull II; Joseph Warren [Bunker Hill]
1760 James Baker [chocolate]; William Hooper [Signer]; Daniel Leonard
1761 [Professor] Samuel Sewall; [Professor] Samuel Williams
1762 Jeremy Belknap [fndr. Mass. Hist. Soc.]; Francis Dana; Elbridge Gerry

1763 Jonathan Bliss [C. Just. N.Brunswick]; Sampson Salter Blowers [C. Just. N.Scotia]; John Jeffries [aeronaut]; Timothy Pickering; Josiah Quincy II ["The Patriot"]
1764 Caleb Strong
1765 Joseph Willard [pres. HC]; Edward Winslow [Supr. Ct N. Brunswick]
1766 [Sir] William Pepperrell
1767 [Sir] Thomas Bernard; Increase Sumner
1768 George Cabot 1766–1768
1769 Theophilus Parsons
1770 Ward Chipman [C. Just. N.Brunswick]; Samuel Osgood [1st US Post. Genl]
1771 James Bowdoin II [Bowdoin College]; Samuel Phillips [Andover Academy]; Winthrop Sargent; [Dr] John Warren
1772 William Eustis [US Secy War]; Levi Lincoln I
1773 John Trumbull
1774 Fisher Ames
1776 Christopher Gore; Royall Tyler
1777 Rufus King
1778 Nathan Dane
1781 Charles Bulfinch; Samuel Dexter [US Secy War & Treas.]
1782 William Dandridge Peck; Stephen Van Rensselaer ["The Good Patroon"]
1783 Harrison Gray Otis
1784 Samuel Webber [pres. HC]
1785 Henry Ware
1786 Isaac Parker [fndr. HLS]
1787 John Quincy Adams; John Murray Forbes [diplomat]
1789 John Thornton Kirkland
1790 Joseph Dennie; Josiah Quincy III [pres. HC; mayor Boston]
1793 Francis Cabot Lowell [Lowell Mills]
1796 John Pickering; James Jackson [MB 1802; MD 1809]
1797 John Collins Warren [surgical anaesthesia]
1798 William Ellery Channing; Joseph Story; Joseph Tuckerman [city missions]
1799 Parker Cleaveland
1800 Washington Allston; Joseph Stevens Buckminster; Timothy Flint; Lemuel Shaw
1802 Levi Lincoln II
1804 Andrews Norton
1806 Jacob Bigelow; Alexander Hill Everett

1811 Edward Everett

1814 Thomas Bulfinch [*Fables*]; William Hickling Prescott; James Walker [Div. Schl; pres. HC]

1815 Thaddeus W. Harris [MD 1820]; John Gorham Palfrey; Jared Sparks [MA in Div. 1819]

1817 George Bancroft; Caleb Cushing [att. HLS]; John Lowell [Lowell Institute]

1821 Robert W. Barnwell; Ralph Waldo Emerson [Div. Schl 1825–1827]; Josiah Quincy IV

1823 Thomas Wilson Dorr; Charles Pickering [MD 1826]; George Ripley [Div. Schl 1826]

1824 Samuel Gridley Howe MD 1824

1825 Charles Francis Adams Sr; Augustus Addison Gould [MD 1830]; Horatio Greenough; Frederic Henry Hedge; John Langdon Sibley

1826 Richard Hildreth; Robert Rantoul

1827 Cornelius C. Felton [pres. HC]; Edmund Quincy

1828 Henry Ingersoll Bowditch [MD 1832]; Robert C. Winthrop

1829 James Freeman Clarke; Benjamin R. Curtis [HLS 1829–1831; US Supr. Ct]; Oliver Wendell Holmes Sr. [MD 1836]; Charles T. Jackson MD 1829; Benjamin Peirce; Charles E. Storrow

1830 Charles Sumner [LLB 1833]

1831 John Lothrop Motley; Wendell Phillips [att. HLS]

1832 Henry W. Bellows [Div. Schl 1837]; John Sullivan Dwight [Div. Schl 1836]; Charles Grafton Page

1833 Francis Bowen; Austin Flint Sr MD 1833; Jeffries Wyman [MD 1837]

1834 William Greenleaf Eliot Div. Schl 1834 [fndr. Washington Univ. St.L.]

1835 Ebenezer Rockwood Hoar [HLS 1839; US Atty-Genl]; Amos Adams Lawrence

1836 Theodore Parker Div. Schl 1836; Jones Very

1837 Henry Jacob Bigelow [MD 1841]; Richard Henry Dana [quits HLS 1840]; Horatio Emmons Hale; Henry David Thoreau

1838 Charles Devens [US Atty-Genl]; James Russell Lowell [LLB 1840]; William Wetmore Story [LLB 1840]; Frederick Goddard Tuckerman 1837–1838 [LLB 1842]

1839 William Maxwell Evarts att. HLS 1838–1839 [US Secy State]; Edward Everett Hale

1840 Elihu Washburne att. HLS 1839–1840 [US Secy State]

1841 Charles A. Dana 1839–1841 [NY *Sun*]; Thomas Wentworth Higginson [Div. Schl 1847]
1843 Thomas Hill [STD 1845; pres. HC]; William Adams Richardson [LLB 1846; Secy Treas.]; Alexander Wheelock Thayer [LLB 1848; biog. Beethoven]
1844 John Call Dalton [MD 1847]; Benjamin Apthorp Gould; Francis Parkman [LLB 1846]
1845 George Phillips Bond; Horace Gray [US Supr. Ct]; Rutherford B. Hayes LLB 1845; William Morris Hunt 1842–1845
1846 Anson Burlingame LLB 1846; Francis J. Child [*Ballads*]; Fitzedward Hall 1842–1846 [Sanskritist]; George Frisbie Hoar [HLS 1849]; George Martin Lane; Charles Eliot Norton
1847 William Crowninshield Endicott [att. HLS; Secy War]
1848 Josiah Parsons Cooke
1849 Christopher Columbus Langdell 1848–1849 [LLB 1853]
1850 Thomas Jefferson Coolidge; Horatio Robinson Storer [MD 1853]
1851 Henry Lee Higginson att. HC August-December 1851; Joseph LeConte; David A. Wells
1852 Horatio Alger [Div. Schl 1860]; Joseph Hodges Choate [LLB 1854]; Ephraim Gurney; James Bradley Thayer [LLB 1856]; William Robert Ware; Chauncey Wright
1853 Charles William Eliot; Austin Flint Jr 1852–1853; William LeBaron Jenney 1852–1853 [1st skyscraper]; Justin Winsor 1849–1853
1854 William E. Chandler LLB 1854 [Secy Navy]; Horace H. Furness; Charles Russell Lowell; Henry Van Brunt
1855 Alexander Agassiz; Francis Channing Barlow; Phillips Brooks; Melville Weston Fuller att. HLS 1854–1855 [C. Just. US Supr. Ct]; Robert Treat Paine [philanthropist]
1856 Charles Francis Adams Jr; James B. Greenough
1857 William Henry Fitzhugh Lee ["Rooney" Lee; s. Robt. E. Lee]; John D. Long [Secy Navy]; John Codman Ropes [LLB 1861]
1858 Henry Adams; Simon Newcomb; Richard Olney LLB 1858; Henry Pickering Walcott
1859 Dorman B. Eaton LLB 1859; John Chipman Gray [LLB 1861]; Charles Sanders Peirce; Henry Hobson Richardson
1860 Henry Billings Brown att. HLS 1859–1860 [US Supr. Ct]; Robert Gould Shaw [Black Regiment]

1861   Henry Pickering Bowditch [MD 1868]; Oliver Wendell
       Holmes Jr [LLB 1866]

1862   Alpheus Hyatt; Edward S. Morse special student 1859–
       1862; Frederic Ward Putnam; Charles Sprague Sargent;
       Nathaniel Southgate Shaler [ScD 1865]

1863   Charles Pickering Bowditch; Jeremiah Curtin; Charles Steb-
       bins Fairchild [LLB 1865; US Secy Treas.]; John Fiske;
       Henry James HLS 1862–1863; William James 1861–1863
       [MD 1869]; J(ohn) Collins Warren [MD 1866]

1864   Reginald Fitz [MD 1868; appendectomy]; Robert Todd Lin-
       coln; Alpheus S. Packard; George Herbert Palmer; William
       C. Whitney HLS 1863–1864 [Secy Navy]

1865   Edward C. Pickering; John Trowbridge [ScD 1873]

1866   William Gilmore Farlow; Charles McBurney ["McBurney's
       point" in appendicitis]; James Jackson Putnam [MD 1870];
       Moorfield Storey

1867   Charles Follen McKim 1866–1867

1868   James Barr Ames [LLB 1872]

1869   William Morris Davis [MD 1870]; Francis Greenwood Pea-
       body [STB 1872]

1870   Brooks Adams

1871   Henry Cabot Lodge I [LLB 1874; PhD 1876]; [Bishop] Wil-
       liam Lawrence

1872   Charles J. Bonaparte [LLB 1874; Secy Navy & US Atty-
       Genl]

1873   J. Lawrence Laughlin [PhD 1876]; Harvey Wiley BS

1874   Ernest Fenollosa; Ulysses S. Grant Jr

1875   Le Baron Russell Briggs [AM 1882]; W. K. Brooks PhD
       1875; Morton Prince [MD 1879]; Denman Ross

1876   Percival Lowell; William Henry Moody [Secy Navy & US
       Atty-Genl; US Supr. Ct]

1877   Louis D. Brandeis LLB 1877; Jutaro Komura LLB 1877
       [For. Min. Japan]; A. Lawrence Lowell [LLB 1880]; Barrett
       Wendell; George E. Woodberry

1878   Edward A. Birge PhD 1878; Edward Channing [PhD 1880];
       G. Stanley Hall PhD 1878; Lucius N. Littauer; Charles Sedg-
       wick Minot ScD 1878

1879   George von Lengerke Meyer [US Post-Genl; Secy Navy];
       Frank William Taussig [PhD 1883]

1880   Robert Bacon [US Secy State]; Albert Bushnell Hart; Theo-
       dore Roosevelt [Nobelist]

Appendix

1881 Francis Ellingwood Abbot PhD 1881; Charles MacVeagh; William Roscoe Thayer

1882 Godfrey Lowell Cabot; Charles Townsend Copeland; Charles Eliot [landscape arch.]; Henry Harland att. Div. Schl 1881–1882 [*Yellow Book*]; George Lyman Kittredge; Owen Wister [AM 1888; LLB 1888]

1883 Joseph Lee [LLB 1887]

1884 John Jay Chapman; Thomas Mott Osborne; [General] Leonard Wood MD 1884

1885 William Randolph Hearst 1883–1885; Benjamin Rand PhD 1885; Logan Pearsall Smith 1884–1885; William Sydney Thayer [MD 1889]

1886 Alanson Bigelow Houghton; Theodore W. Richards [PhD 1888; Nobelist]; George Santayana [PhD 1889]

1887 George Pierce Baker; Bern[h]ard Berenson; Archibald Cary Coolidge; Mark DeWolfe Howe I [AM 1888]; George H. Parker [ScD 1891]; James Harvey Robinson [AM 1888]

1888 Charles Francis Adams [LLB 1892; Secy Navy]; James Loeb [Loeb Classical Library]; George Herbert Mead; Wallace C. Sabine AM 1888

1889 Irving Babbitt [AM 1893]; Richard Clarke Cabot [MD 1892]; Charles B. Davenport [PhD 1892]; J. Pierpont Morgan Jr; George A. Reisner [PhD 1893]; Henry L. Stimson AM 1889 [HLS 1889–1890]; Robert DeCourcy Ward [AM 1893]; Charles Warren [AM 1892; HLS 1889–1892]

1890 W. E. B. Du Bois [PhD 1895]; Norman Hapgood; Robert Herrick; Sidney Mezes [PhD 1893; dir. Wilson's "Inquiry" 1917–1918]; Roscoe Pound HLS 1889–1890

1891 Nicholas Longworth; William Lyon Phelps AM 1891; Robert Williams Wood

1892 James Rowland Angell AM 1892; W. Cameron Forbes; Hutchins Hapgood [AM 1897]; Thomas W. Lamont; Henrietta Leavitt [Radcliffe]; Robert Morss Lovett; Guy Lowell

1893 William E. Castle [PhD 1895]; Learned Hand [LLB 1896]; William Vaughn Moody [AM 1894]; Paul Elmer More AM 1893; Vernon L. Parrington; Edwin Arlington Robinson 1891–1893; Oswald Garrison Villard

1894 Augustus Hand LLB 1894; Edward Burlingame Hill; Fredderick Law Olmsted Jr; Edward K. Rand [AM 1895; Div. Schl 1894–1895]

1895 Harvey Cushing MD 1895; Edward Waldo Forbes; Seihin

Ikeda [gov. Bank of Japan]; Elliott Joslin MD 1895; Trumbull Stickney; (William) Monroe Trotter [AM 1896]

1896 Walter Bradford Cannon [AM 1897; MD 1900]; Reginald Daly PhD 1896; Sidney B. Fay [PhD 1900]; Edwin B. Holt [PhD 1901]; Herbert Spencer Jennings PhD 1896; Gilbert N. Lewis [PhD 1899]; Roger Bigelow Merriman [PhD 1902]; John Lord O'Brian; John R. Swanton [PhD 1900]; Edward L. Thorndike [AM 1897]

1897 Roland B. Dixon [PhD 1900]; Arthur O. Lovejoy AM 1897; Theodore Lyman [PhD 1900; "Lyman lines" in spectroscopy]; Percy Mackaye; Elmer E. Southard [MD 1901; AM 1902]; Gertrude Stein 1893–1897 [Radcliffe]; Percy S. Straus [Macy's]; Robert S. Woodworth AM 1897

1898 Oakes Ames [AM 1899; botanist]; Lawrence J. Henderson [MD 1902]; James Hazen Hyde; Robert M. Yerkes [PhD 1902]

1899 Herbert Croly 1886–1887, 1895–1899; James D. Dole [pineapples]; Robert Frost 1897–1899; Robert E. Park AM 1899; Ralph Barton Perry PhD 1899; W. H. Sheldon PhD 1899

1900 Robert Woods Bliss; William R. Castle; Benton Mackaye [AM (Forestry) 1905]; Edward Mallinckrodt Jr [AM 1901]; William Phillips; Ralph Pulitzer; Paul Sachs; Wallace Stevens 1897–1900; Alfred Marston Tozzer [PhD 1904]; Oswald Veblen

1901 Henry Bryant Bigelow [PhD 1906]; Payne Whitney LLB 1901

1902 Witter Bynner; Joseph C. Grew

1903 Knight Dunlap PhD 1903

1904 Arthur A. Ballantine [LLB 1907]; Percy W. Bridgman [PhD 1908; Nobelist]; John Haynes Holmes STB 1904; Helen Keller [Radcliffe]; Chandler R. Post [PhD 1909]; Franklin Delano Roosevelt

1905 Roger Baldwin [ACLU]; Hiram Bingham PhD 1905 [disc. Machu Picchu]; George D. Birkhoff [AM 1906]; John Livingston Lowes PhD 1905; Ogden Mills [LLB 1907; Secy Treas.]; Lothrop Stoddard [PhD 1914]

1906 Thomas Barbour [PhD 1910]; Morris R. Cohen PhD 1906; Abraham Flexner AM 1906; Felix Frankfurter LLB 1906; Clarence I. Lewis [PhD 1910]; Vilhjalmur Stefansson Div. Schl 1903–1904, GSAS 1904–1906

1907   Earl Derr Biggers [Charlie Chan]; John Gould Fletcher
       1903–1907; Leland Harrison; John A. Lomax AM 1907;
       Maxwell Evarts Perkins; Harry Elkins Widener

1908   George Biddle; Van Wyck Brooks; Horace M. Kallen PhD
       1908; A. V. Kidder [PhD 1914]; George Richards Minot
       [MD 1912; Nobelist]; Samuel Eliot Morison [PhD 1912];
       Syngman Rhee AM 1908 [pres. Korea]; Henry M. Sheffer
       PhD 1908 ["Sheffer's stroke" in logic]; John Hall Wheelock;
       Paul Dudley White [MD 1911]

1909   Roger Adams [PhD 1912]; Francis Biddle [LLB 1911]; El-
       liott Cutler [MD 1913]; T. S. Eliot [AM 1910; GSAS 1911–
       1914; Nobelist]; H. V. Kaltenborn; William Lyon Macken-
       zie King PhD 1909; Lee Simonson

1910   Heywood Broun 1906–1910; Stuart Chase; Bronson Cut-
       ting; William Francis Gibbs 1906–1910 [designer Liberty
       Ships]; William C. Graustein [AM 1911]; Robert Edmond
       Jones; Walter Lippmann; Clarence C. Little [ScD 1914];
       John Reed; Alan Seeger; James B. Sumner [PhD 1914;
       Nobelist]

1911   Alan Gregg [MD 1916]; Charles Howard McIlwain PhD
       1911; Harry A. Wolfson ["as of" 1912; PhD 1915]

1912   George Abbott special student 1912; Conrad Aiken; Freder-
       ick Lewis Allen [AM 1913]; Joseph Patrick Kennedy; Alfred
       Lee Loomis LLB 1912; Fan Noli [Prime Minister Albania];
       Carter G. Woodson PhD 1912

1913   Robert A. Benchley; Zechariah Chafee Jr LLB 1913; James
       Bryant Conant [PhD 1916]; Harold Stearns; Norbert Wiener
       PhD 1913

1914   Thurman Arnold LLB 1914; William C. Bullitt HLS 1913–
       1914; John P. Marquand; Leverett Saltonstall [LLB 1917];
       Sumner Welles

1915   E. E. Cummings [AM 1916]; R. Buckminster Fuller 1913–
       1915; Christian Herter; William L. Langer [PhD 1923];
       George Wilhelm Merck [pharmaceuticals]; Henry A. Mur-
       ray; Eugene O'Neill special student 1914–1915 [Nobelist];
       Robert P. Patterson LLB 1915; John Rock [MD 1918];
       Roger Sessions; T. V. Soong; Edward C. Tolman PhD 1915;
       Sewell Wright ScD 1915

1916   S. N. Behrman; Samuel Flagg Bemis PhD 1916; Benjamin
       Cohen SJD 1916; John Dos Passos; Hetty Goldman PhD

1916 [Radcliffe]; Sidney Howard special student 1915–1916

1917 Brooks Atkinson; Robert Hillyer; James Paul Warburg

1918 Dean Acheson LLB 1918; Bernard DeVoto; Donald F. Jones ScD 1918; Alain Locke PhD 1918; Robert E. Sherwood ["as of," att. 1914–1917]

1919 Gordon Allport [PhD 1922]; Lawrence Dennis ["as of " 1920; Fascist]; Robert Frederick Loeb MD 1919; Archibald MacLeish LLB 1919; Helen Taussig 1917–1919 [Radcliffe]

1920 Malcolm Cowley; John Cowles ["as of" 1921]; Merle Curti [PhD 1927]; Leslie C. Dunn ScD 1920; Alfred C. Kinsey ScD 1920; Susanne Knauth (Langer) [Radcliffe; PhD 1926]; William P. Murphy MD 1920 [Nobelist]; [Admiral] Isoroku Yamamoto special student 1919–1920 [Pearl Harbor]

1921 Brand Blanshard PhD 1921; Paul C. Cabot; Thomas S. Lamont; John J. McCloy LLB 1921; Ogden Nash 1920–1921

1922 Edgar Anderson PhD 1922; Philip Barry special student 1919–1922; John Nicholas Brown; Donald Culross Peattie; Virgil Thomson; John H. Van Vleck PhD 1922 [Nobelist]; Thomas Wolfe AM 1922

1923 John T. Edsall [MD 1928]; Granville Hicks [AM 1929]; Percy L. Julian AM 1923; Donald Oenslager; John C. Slater PhD 1923; Shields Warren MD 1923

1924 Leonard Carmichael PhD 1924; James Gould Cozzens 1922–1924; Louis F. Fieser PhD 1924; Sheldon Glueck PhD 1924; Henry-Russell Hitchcock [AM 1927]; Charles Huggins MD 1924 [Nobelist]; Oliver La Farge [AM 1929]; Corliss Lamont; Henry Cabot Lodge II; F. S. C. Northrop PhD 1924; Walter Piston; Cornelius P. Rhoads MD 1924; Adlai Stevenson II HLS 1922–1924

1925 Thomas G. Corcoran LLB 1925; Gardner Cowles; Stanley Marcus [HBS 1926; Neiman-Marcus]; Neil H. McElroy; Robert S. Mulliken Postdoctoral Fell. 1923–1925 [Nobelist] J. Robert Oppenheimer; Cecilia Payne [-Gaposchkin] PhD 1925 [Radcliffe]

1926 Countee Cullen AM 1926; Stanley Kunitz [AM 1927]

1927 Philip Bard PhD 1927; Charles E. Bohlen; F. O. Matthiessen PhD 1927; Gregory Pincus ScD 1927 [The Pill]

1928 Barry Bingham; Nelson Goodman [PhD 1941]; Herbert Hoover Jr MBA 1928; Mark DeWolfe Howe II [LLB 1933];

Edwin Land 1927–1928; Nathan Marsh Pusey [PhD 1937]; George D. Snell [ScD 1930; Nobelist]

1929 Harry Andrew Blackmun [LLB 1932; US Supr. Ct]; John King Fairbank; Alger Hiss LLB 1929; Robert C. Weaver [PhD 1934; US Secy Housing]; Paul Weiss PhD 1929

1930 Elliott Carter; John F. Enders PhD 1930 [Nobelist]; William Henry Hastie LLB 1930 [SJD 1933]; Philip Johnson [B. Arch. 1943]; Lincoln Kirstein

1931 William Joseph Brennan LLB 1931 [US Supr. Ct]; Hadley Cantril PhD 1931; Paul Freund LLB 1931; David Riesman; B. F. Skinner PhD 1931

1932 James Agee; C. Douglas Dillon; Lewis F. Powell Jr LLM 1932 [US Supr. Ct]; Willard Van Orman Quine PhD 1932; W. Barry Wood Jr

1933 Richard Eberhart GSAS 1932–1933; Harry Levin [Soc. Fells 1934–1939]; Wilbur Mills HLS 1930–1933; William H. Stein [Nobelist]; S. S. Stevens PhD 1933; Barbara Wertheim (Tuchman) [Radcliffe]

1934 Ralph H. Bunche PhD 1934 [Nobelist]; Archibald Cox [LLB 1937]

1935 Daniel J. Boorstin; Francis D. Moore [MD 1938]

1936 William S. Burroughs [*Naked Lunch*]; Donald O. Hebb PhD 1936; Robert K. Merton PhD 1936; David Rockefeller; E. Bright Wilson Soc. Fells 1934–1936

1937 Robert Lowell 1935–1937; Edmund Sears Morgan [PhD 1942]; Gerard Piel; Delmore Schwartz 1935–1937; Lewis Thomas MD 1937; Peter Viereck [PhD 1942]

1938 John Bardeen Soc. Fells 1935–1938 [Nobelist 1956, 1972]; Donald Griffin [PhD 1942]; Edward Mills Purcell PhD 1938 [Nobelist]; Pete Seeger 1936–1938; Arthur M. Schlesinger Jr [Soc. Fells 1939–1942]; Caspar Weinberger [LLB 1941]; Theodore White; Robert Burns Woodward Postdoctoral Fell. 1938 [Soc. Fells 1938–1940; Nobelist]

1939 Howard Aiken PhD 1939; Walter Jackson Bate [PhD 1942]; Leonard Bernstein; James Laughlin; Robert S. McNamara MBA 1939; Edwin Reischauer PhD 1939; James Tobin [PhD 1947; Soc. Fells 1947–1950; Nobelist]; Stanislaw Ulam Soc. Fells 1936–1939 [hydrogen bomb]

1940 Oscar Handlin PhD 1940; John Fitzgerald Kennedy; Alan Jay Lerner; William Proxmire MBA 1940 [MPA 1948]; Donald Regan; Frederick C. Robbins MD 1940 [Nobelist]; Thomas H. Weller MD 1940 [Nobelist]

1941 Jerome Bruner PhD 1941; John Hope Franklin PhD 1941; Elliot Lee Richardson [LLB 1947]; Paul Samuelson PhD 1941 [Nobelist]; Howard Nemerov

1942 William French Smith LLB 1942 [US Atty-Genl]

1943 Philip W. Anderson [PhD 1949; Nobelist]; Christian Anfinsen PhD 1943 [Nobelist]; Thomas S. Kuhn SB [Soc. Fells 1948–1952; PhD 1949]; Norman Mailer; Andreas Papandreou PhD 1943; S. Dillon Ripley PhD 1943 [Smithsonian]

1945 Pierre Elliott Trudeau AM 1945

1946 William T. Coleman Jr LLB 1946 [US Secy Transportation]; Daniel Carleton Gajdusek MD 1946 [Nobelist]; Adam Ulam PhD 1947; Richard Wilbur [Soc. Fells 1947–1950]

1948 Kingman Brewster LLB 1948; Robert Francis Kennedy; An Wang PhD 1948 [magnetic memory core]

1949 John Ashbery; John Hawkes; William H. Rehnquist AM 1949 [US Supr. Ct]

1950 Robert Bly; Henry Kissinger [PhD 1954; Nobelist]; Luna Leopold PhD 1950; Ben R. Mottelson PhD 1950 [Nobelist]; Richard Pipes PhD 1950; James R. Schlesinger [PhD 1956]

1951 John Cowles Jr; Harold Furth [PhD 1960; fusion energy]; Richard C. Lewontin; Adrienne Rich [Radcliffe]

1952 Edward Seaga [Prime Minister Jamaica]; Adlai Stevenson III [LLB 1957]

1953 Bernard Bailyn PhD 1953; Zbigniew Brzezinski PhD 1953; Walter Gilbert [AM 1954; Nobelist]; Bernard F. Law [Cardinal Boston]

1954 Derek Curtis Bok LLB 1954; Richard Lyman PhD 1954; John Updike

1955 Clifford L. Alexander Jr; Noam Chomsky Soc. Fells 1951–1955; (An)Drew Lewis MBA 1955 [US Secy Transportation]; Edward O. Wilson PhD 1955 [Soc. Fells 1953–1956]

1956 J(ohn) Carter Brown [MBA 1958]; Clifford Geertz PhD 1956; Edward Moore Kennedy; Kenneth G. Wilson [Soc. Fells 1956–1962; Nobelist]

1957 Andrew Brimmer PhD 1957; Hanna Holborn Gray PhD 1957; Donald Hodel [US Secy Energy]

1958 Sheldon Glashow PhD 1958 [Nobelist]; Aga Khan; Ralph Nader LLB 1958

1959 Arthur Kopit

1960 Elizabeth Hanford (Dole) MA in Ed. 1960 [JD 1965; US Secy Transportation]

1961 John Davison Rockefeller IV
1962 Roald Hoffmann PhD 1962 [Soc. Fells 1962–1965; Nobel-
      ist]; Elizabeth Holtzmann [Radcliffe; JD 1965]; Marquess of
      Tavistock [heir to 13th Duke of Bedford]
1963 Pierre S. Du Pont LLB 1963
1964 Harrison Schmitt PhD 1964 [astronaut]
1965 Miguel de la Madrid (Hurtado) MPA 1965 [pres. Mexico]
1967 Howard Georgi
1971 William John Bennett JD 1971 [US Secy Educ.]
1976 Yo Yo Ma

Some Harvard Faculty and Staff Members

with no earned Harvard degrees,
arranged by first year of service

1783 Benjamin Waterhouse 1783–1812
1819 George Ticknor 1819–1833
1825 Karl/Charles Follen 1825–1835
1832 Karl/Charles Beck 1832–1850
1835 William Cranch Bond 1835–1859
      Henry Wadsworth Longfellow 1835–1854
1842 Asa Gray 1842–1888
      Evangelinus Apostolides Sophocles 1842–1883
1848 Louis Agassiz 1848–1873
1862 John Knowles Paine 1862–1905
1863 Charles-Edouard Brown-Séquard 1863–1865
1880 Charles R. Lanman 1880–1926
1882 Josiah Royce 1882–1916
1884 Kuno Francke 1884–1917
1888 Charles Gross 1888–1909
1892 [Sir] William Ashley 1892–1901
1896 Annie Jump Cannon 1896–1941 (HC Observatory)
      Theobald Smith 1896–1915
1902 Charles Homer Haskins 1902–1931
      Arthur E. Kennelly 1902–1930 [Kennelly-Heaviside Layer]
1908 William Scott Ferguson 1908–1945
      William Morton Wheeler 1908–1937
1910 Frederick Jackson Turner 1910–1924
1912 David L. Edsall 1912–1935

1914   Edward Murray East 1914–1938
       Kirsopp Lake 1914–1938
1916   Harold J. Laski 1916–1920
1919   Alice Hamilton 1919–1935
1920   William McDougall 1920–1927
1921   Harlow Shapley 1921–1956
1922   Edwin J. Cohn 1922–1953
1923   Hans Zinsser 1923–1940
1924   A. Kingsley Porter 1924–1933
       Alfred North Whitehead 1924–1936
1926   Elton Mayo 1926–1947
1927   Michael Karpovich 1927–1957
1928   [Sir] Charles K. Webster 1928–1932
1930   George Kistiakowsky 1930–1971
       Milman Parry 1930–1935
       Pitirim Sorokin 1930–1964
1931   Wassily Leontief 1931–1975 (Nobelist)
       Perry Miller 1931–1963
1932   Joseph Schumpeter 1932–1950
1934   J. K. Galbraith tutor 1934–1939; professor 1949–1975
       George Wald 1934–1977 (Nobelist)
1937   Heinrich Brüning 1937–1952
       Karl S. Lashley 1937–1958
       Jakob Rosenberg 1937–1964
1938   Marcel Breuer 1938–1946
       Walter Gropius 1938–1952
       John Dunlop 1938–   (US Secy Labor)
1939   Werner Jaeger 1939–1961
1941   Tilly Edinger 1941–1964 (MCZ)
       Fritz Lipman 1941–1957 (Nobelist)
1944   I. A. Richards 1944–1963
1945   John Berryman 1945–1949
       Julian Schwinger 1945–1972 (Nobelist)
1947   Georg von Békésy 1947–1966 (Nobelist)
1948   Helen Maud Cam 1948–1954
       Alexander Gerschenkron 1948–1975
1949   Nicolaas Bloembergen 1949–   (Nobelist)
       Roman Jakobson 1949–1967
1951   McGeorge Bundy 1951–1961
       [Sir] Geoffrey Wilkinson 1951–1956 (Nobelist) denied tenure

1953   Ernst Mayr 1953–1975
José Luis Sert 1958–1969
1954   Konrad Bloch 1954–1982 (Nobelist)
1955   Sir Hamilton Gibb 1955–1964
Paul Tillich 1955–1962
J. D. Watson 1955–1976 (Nobelist)
1959   Edward C. Banfield 1959–1972; 1976–
David Hubel 1959–　(Nobelist)
Stephen Kuffler 1959–1980
William N. Lipscomb 1959–　(Nobelist)
George Gaylord Simpson 1959–1970
Torsten Wiesel 1959–　(Nobelist)
1960   Erik Erikson 1960–1970
Simon Kuznets 1960–1971 (Nobelist)
1962   John Rawls 1962–
1965   Robert Nozick 1965–1967; 1969–
1968   Kenneth J. Arrow 1968–1979 (Nobelist)
1970   Baruj Benacerraf 1970–　(Nobelist)
Carlo Rubbia 1970–　(Nobclist)
1973   Steven Weinberg 1973–　(Nobelist)